Sons of Heaven Brothers of Nature: The Naxi of Southwest China

Pedro Ceinos
Arcones

Pedro Ceinos Arcones,

Editing: Roger Casas

Design: Karim Nimri.

Front cover drawing: He Zhiben

Map: Wei Hua

Dongba Characters: Yang Xiaohui (Edongba)

Contents

4. Naxi Culture 130

5. Naxi life cycle   150

6. Naxi Yearly cycle   184

Acknowledgments

Most of the intellectual inspirers of this work are mentioned in the bibliographic section. Here I want to express my thanks to other persons whose collaboration was very helpful during my field trips and the process of writing this book. Dongba He Zhiben of Baishuitai devoted part of his precious time to describe their main ceremonies to me once and again, patiently explaining their main divination techniques, showing me his sacred tools, and allowing me to take pictures at will, of him and his family. The assistance of his son He Yufu, and his daughter in law Xiu Hua, who made clear to me the obscure points of He Zhiben talks, has been precious. His grandson He Lidou acted as improvised guide to Baishuitai terraces. They generously allowed me to use in this book some of the fine Dongba paintings of He Zhiben. Mr. He Shurong, also from Baidi, helped me understand the local differences between the Naheng and the Rerke branches of the Naxi, as well as the origin and transformation of the Alili music and dance. Conversations with Dongba He Jihua, of Mingyin, helped me understand the sacred geography of the Naxi, the present situation of the Dongbas, as well as the importance of environmental preservation among them.

My friend Constantin de Slizewicz offered me his valuable collection of Naxi pictures. Sam Mitchell provided important suggestions about the book; here I want to express a posthumous homage to him. He Yumei, the owner of the Zen Garden Hotel in Lijiang, and He Zhengyuan, the caretaker of the former residence of Joseph F. Rock in Yuhu, both Naxi, encouraged me to write this book. Nightly talks with John Israel have been useful for this work. Roger Casas and Gonzalo Pavillard have made important contributions in the final steps of this book.

My special thanks to Mr. Yang Xiaohui, the creator of the E-Dongba software for the input of Dongba pictographs. I am sure that without his work this book would not be as interesting as we hope. Edongba software can be downloaded from http://www.zmnsoft.com/edongba/En/

Introduction

Hidden in the confines of East Asia, where the imposing mountains of the eastern foothills of the Himalayas blocked for centuries the western expansion of the Chinese, there is a natural border between China, Tibet and Southeast Asia; a geographical, natural and ethnic divide that effectively separates three worlds: Three fascinating ways of understand life, death, and the time between. This frontier was inhabited by a nation of ancient ancestry that during centuries kept a close relationship with a heterogeneous group of tribes and empires, giving origin to one of the most remarkable cultures on earth. They are the Naxi people.

Though the origin of the Naxi civilization is lost in the mists of time, its culture developed slowly during the last thousand years to become the key to understand the cultural mosaic of the Sino-Tibetan borderlands. In the process they experienced amazing splendors and witnessed their political fall; the culture developed along this tortuous road remained unknown to the outside world until the middle decades of the 20th century, when the curtain opened for a while, letting the world catch a sight of a mysterious civilization. Before a real understanding of their inner life could be grasped, the curtain closed again.

The Naxi occupy a central position in the research and understanding of the old traditions of East Asia as no other ethnic group can claim. To their Qiang ancestry and the cultural influences of other Loloish[1] groups that live in their neighbourhood, their culture incorporated elements of the oldest Tibetan culture, influences of the Mongolian and through them of Central and North Asian civilizations, and a repository of ideas and traditions that can be traced back to the archaic culture of China. No other ethnic group of Asia has preserved so rich and multifaceted ancient heritage, no other ethnic group is so central to the research of the old cultures of Asia. The role of the Naxi as preservers of ancient cultural heritages can be attributed to the isolation of some communities and to the writing of a surprising amount of sacred books, maybe thousands of them treasured in the hands of their religious specialists, known to the outside world as the Dongba Classics. The study of Naxi traditions has changed the cultural meaning of the Sino-Tibetan borderlands, with their main elements ranked as intangible cultural heritages, and Lijiang recognized as a site where the main civilizations of East Asia intersected and integrated, creating an original and diverse culture.

Living in a time characterized by a materialistic view of the world, it can be surprising to discover how in the description of Naxi culture, the spiritual world is continuously present, with the influence of gods and demons always at hand, and a feeling of sacredness permeating their ideas about man and nature. These beliefs of the Naxi originated in two main

---

[1] Loloish or Yi groups are those ethnic groups related with the present day Yi nationality, formerly known as Lolo, Nuoso and other ethonims.

myths that will be discussed in this book, one emphasizing the brotherhood of humans and nature, and the other the divine origin of human beings. Together they provide the ideological structure that serves as the basis of Naxi religion and culture. Central to Naxi cultural life are the Dongba priests, resourceful artists and mediators between the human and divine worlds, whose traditions can be credited with some of the most brilliant creations in the human history: the invention and use of a pictographic language, the writing of more than 20.000 sacred scriptures in this script, the creation of long scroll paintings more than 15-meter long, and the development of an ancient dance notation.

After the Naxi territory was opened to the outside world in the 1980s, an interesting amount of books and academic papers have been published about the most remarkable features of their life, culture and religion. Unfortunately, most of these publications, written in Chinese, are not available to the general reader, as are neither the handful of academic studies full of technical terms difficult to understand to the non-initiated, or the simple and well illustrated tourist books, more suited to be considered a souvenir than a tool to get a deeper understanding of Naxi culture.

Every year thousands of travelers from all around the world visit the Naxi region, turning their former isolation in a permanent exhibition of their lands and homes. During their stay in Lijiang they get in contact with some of the most outstanding characteristics of Naxi culture: Dongba pictographs, Old City traditional architecture, Alili popular dance, ethnic clothes, Baisha mural paintings, Dongjing music,

13

etc., but unfortunately these dispersed manifestations of the Naxi culture fail to provide an overall understanding of the Naxi people, remaining instead as touristic activities without a link to the soul of the people who created them, and part of whose spiritual world they are.

This first and sudden contact with the Naxi culture arises the interest of many travelers that unfortunately cannot find any materials with whom satiate their thirst. This book was written to fill this void. Blending the most interesting Chinese and western academic materials in an easily readable and understandable guide to Naxi culture and history, we want to let the outside world understand the human environment of Lijiang, to help the travelers fully enjoy their visit to the lands of the Naxi, and to provide our readers a permanent emotional link to one of the most fascinating ethnic groups on Earth: The Naxi.

This book is structured in six main chapters, "The Naxi of Southwest China" is an overview of Naxi geographical and natural environment, Naxi population and territorial distribution, language and especially Dongba pictographs, the only pictographic writing still in use in the world, that was developed by the Dongba priests as a route guide to their religious ceremonies; "Echoes from the past: Naxi History" shows a chronological description of the history and social development of the Naxi people, from the oldest information about them that can be found in Chinese chronicles, to their royal genealogies and the 20th century changes that shattered their traditional world; "Gods and Dongbas: Naxi religion" is an overall description of the main aspects of Naxi traditional religion, introducing the religious beliefs of the Naxi, their view of nature as a sacred entity, the features of the Dongba and *Lhubu* priests, their main deities and the ceremonies performed to honor them. In "Naxi Culture" the basic aspects of the material culture of the Naxi are described, the symbolism of the village, home and dress, as well as the special characteristics of their society. In "Naxi life cycle" the three main stages in the life of each Naxi: birth, pairing, and death, are discussed. In "Naxi yearly cycle" the reader will find information about the festivals and ceremonies usually celebrated on a yearly basis, discovering also in the ritual celebration of the year interesting influences of diverse origin. The last chapter "Music, Arts, and Literature" is a short exposition of the way the Naxi people expressed in both the secular and profane realms, their rich spiritual world; their different artistic traditions related to music, art and literature are described, and their more acclaimed artistic works are introduced.

Not aimed to give an overall description of Naxi culture and religion but a comprehensive guide to the most remarkable features of them, we think that this book can be an ideal introduction to further research, a useful companion of travel and an indispensable tool in the cultural elaboration that follows man adventures in faraway lands.

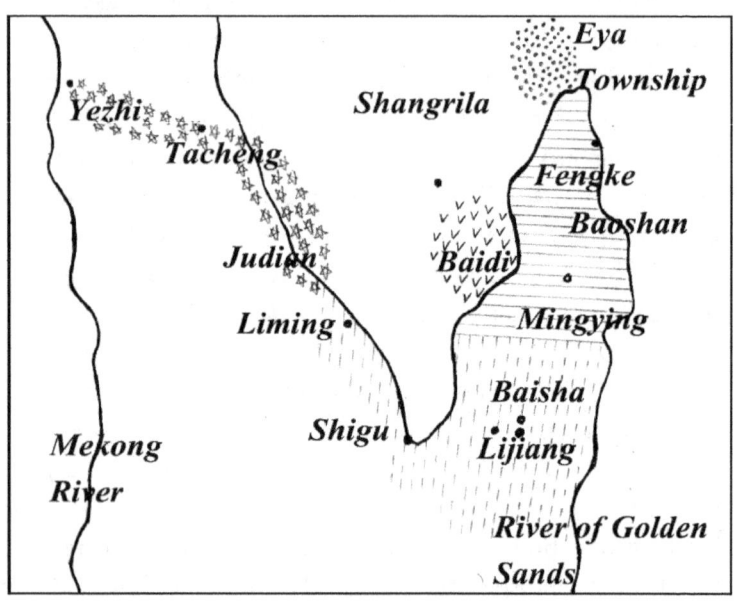

Map of the distribution of the Naxi people with their five main ethno-geographical regions.

CHAPTER 1

The Naxi of Southwest China

The Naxi[2] are the most charismatic ethnic group of China; their culture preserves a set of special characteristics that make them one of the more interesting peoples of our planet, including the preservation of the only pictographic script still in use, and the religion associated with it, the development of a philosophy that stresses the respect and conservation of nature, the matrilineal tendencies of their society, and the ability to preserve old cultural traditions already disappeared elsewhere. Anthony Jackson considers that "this peculiar combination of attributes makes them unique, not only among the various ethnic minorities that inhabit southern China, but also in the ethnographic record" (1976: 28).

Population and location

---

[2] Also called Na-khi, Nakhi, Moso, Mo-so, etc. See the Glossary for Naxi terms and different Western transliterations.

The Naxi ethnic minority has a population of about 280,000[3]. Most of them live in communities in the northwest of Yunnan Province, in Yulong Naxi Autonomous County and Lijiang Old City, the rest being scattered in Weixi, Shangrila[4], Ninglang, Deqin, Yongsheng, Heqing, Jianchuan and Lanping counties in Yunnan Province, Muli County in Sichuan Province and Mangkang County of the Tibet Autonomous Region (Ma Yin: 1989). The distribution of the Naxi people has a half-star shape with the center in the City of Lijiang; it reflects the conquering expeditions of the Naxi kings in their pursue to expand their domains (and the Chinese imperial territory) to the west. So, while the southern and eastern limits of the Naxi occupation have been more or less stable, their western dispersion follows the river valleys to lands as distant as Eya in Muli County, Mangkang County in Tibet, or Yezhi in the Upper Mekong River. This is because Naxi garrisons were deployed in every new territory conquered by their kings to act as guardians of the new border. There they multiplied and build their homes, becoming an outpost of the Naxi culture.

The Naxi, living in the border between the Chinese and Tibetan worlds, inhabit mainly but not exclusively the lowlands and the valleys among the mountain ridges[5], leaving most of the mountainous territory to the Pumi (in the east) and

---

[3] As the Chinese censuses usually include together the population of the Naxi and Moso minorities, we take out from the estimated Naxi population of 310.000 in the 2000 year census, about 30.000 Moso people.

[4] Formerly known as Zhongdian.

[5] Though there are also villages in the mountains, and mountains have an economic, cultural and symbolic importance to the Naxi, even in the mountainous regions Naxi prefer to live in the lowlands.

the Lisu (in the west), possibly the original inhabitants of these regions, and to the Yi and Miao, more recent migrants. In the urban centers a good number of people from the Bai nationality as well as Han Chinese, can be found. Bai traders and artisans are very famous among the Naxi. Han Chinese, on their side, started to migrate to Naxi lands about 600 years ago, when the Mu kings keep a close relation with Ming emperors. Early migrants have been already integrated in Naxi society. The political, economical and cultural center of the Naxi is Lijiang. An old city lying under the shadow of the imposing Jade Dragon Snow Mountain, Lijiang is located approximately in the center of the biggest plains inhabited by them. Lijiang Old City is the capital of the Lijiang Municipality, which with a total area of 21,219 square kilometers comprises also four counties: Yulong Naxi Autonomous County, Ninglang Yi Autonomous County, Yongsheng County, and Huaping County. In 2003 the population of Lijiang Municipality was 1,118,835 inhabitants[6]; among them the main aboriginal nationalities, the Naxi, Yi, Lisu and Pumi, make up only about a 30% of the total population (Zhang and He 2005: 1-4). The growing population, most of them migrants recently arrived from other provinces of China in the wave of the tourism development, is diluting the Naxi presence in their own lands. Real estate development, relying on the seductive character of the region, is expanding the city area at an alarming speed, as more and more people choose Lijiang as a second residence. As

---

[6] This figure should be considered to refer only to permanent residents. As the dramatic increase of the tourism industry carries every year millions of visitors and thousands of short-term residents, it is difficult to calculate the exact population at any given moment.

a reflection of these demographic changes, in 2003, the former Lijiang Naxi Autonomous County was divided into Lijiang Old City District, a cosmopolitan urban center that has become one of the main touristic attractions of China, and Yulong Naxi Autonomous County, that with a total area of 6,392 square kilometers (95% of it mountainous area and foothills) is now the only Naxi autonomous county in China. Among the 209,710 inhabitants of Yulong County, only 119,330 are Naxi, representing 57,39% of the total population (Zhang and He 2005: 19).

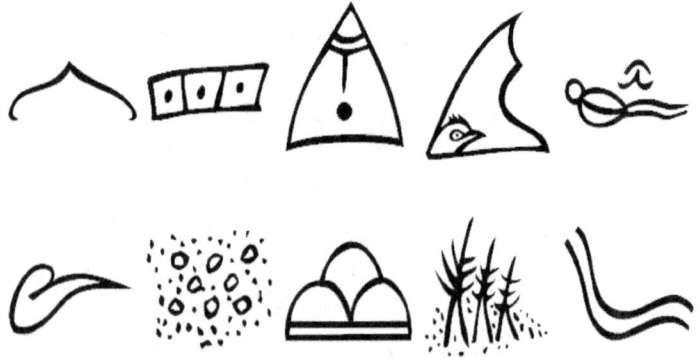

Geographical accidents in Dongba pictographs; from left to right: heaven (the vault of heaven), earth, mountain, cliff (a mountain broken), river, lake, sands (many small stones), stone, forest (three, many trees), and road.

The Naxi territory can be defined by the continuous presence of the powerful Yangtze River, locally known as the River of Golden Sands, as its sands have been mined from old times due to their high content of gold. From its origin in the grasslands of Qinghai province, the Yangtze River runs in a south-southeast direction down to Shigu, where, blocked by mountains, it turns suddenly northeast, leaving at the east the heart of Naxi territory. North of Fengke the river turns toward the south again, this time separating Naxi from Moso territory. After a new turn it runs northeast and traversing Sichuan Province, eastwards to the Yellow Sea. Separating the Naxi from the Tibetan in the west and from the Moso in the east, the banks of the river were also a natural road to the expansion of the Naxi people. The River of Golden Sands and the tributaries that irrigate the Naxi lands, open their way cutting trough impressing mountain ranges, of which the Jade Dragon Mountain is the most outstanding, with uplands that rise sometimes abruptly to reach a maximum height of 5,400 meters, a contrast with river valleys where altitude is a little more than 1,200 meters above sea level. Villages usually lie in the river valleys while on the alpine meadows yak are grazed and barley is grown on suitable level spots (Jackson 1976: 13).

Climate experiences seasonal variations with differences that reflect altitude and geographical conditions; it varies from cold and temperate in the highlands to subtropical in the river valleys. Rainfall is plentiful, especially in July and August. Agriculture is the main occupation of the Naxi people. The chief crops are wheat, rice, maize, potatoes, beans, hemp and cotton. The bend of the Yangtze River is heavily forested, Jade Dragon Mountain is known as a "flora storehouse"; its dense forests contain Chinese fir, Korean pine, Yunnan pine and other valuable trees, as well as many varieties of herbs and fungus used for centuries to make medicines. The mountains and forests around Lijiang have been a natural reserve for many animal species. The detailed knowledge of the local wild fauna and flora showed in the Dongba manuscripts is a good basis to a better understanding of the importance of this region to the preservation of many endemic species. Tigers, leopards, bears, wild boars, as well as local varieties of deer and goats, roamed freely on these mountains until the middle of the 20th century. Except for tigers, most of these animals can still be found in the pristine forests of the Jade Snow Mountain. There are rich reserves of gold, mined in some parts of the river to our days, silver, copper, and other metals. The Naxi developed interesting production techniques, being specially appreciated their copper wares and leather products. Trading expeditions led Naxi merchants to distant lands in Tibet and India, and make their products well known in a region even wider.

Naxi Human geography

The complicated geography of the Naxi territory gave origin to interesting regional variations among the people. We can roughly divide their land in five ethno-geographical areas: Lijiang City and the central plains, Baidi and the territory that connects to the Tibetan world, Ludian and the lands that lead to the Mekong River, Baoshan and the northern territories, and the isolated communities of Eya. We don't include here the Moso and related peoples because, though a common origin of both Naxi and Moso could be traced, at present they show so many cultural differences as to consider them two distinctive ethnic entities.

1. Lijiang and the central plains.

The Naxi living in Lijiang City and surrounding areas are the best known to the outside world; their culture and traditions, however, have been deeply influenced by Chinese culture, specially after 1723, when the incorporation of Lijiang to the Chinese empire was accompanied by a constant migration of Chinese males that, marrying local women, created a border society that included cultural elements extracted from both the Naxi and Chinese cultural realms. The rich agricultural valleys surrounding Lijiang Old City are the economic and political center of the Naxi, the first place where they settled and the home from where they expanded their territory. Baisha, a cluster of villages 10 kilometers north of Lijiang, was the ritual center of the Mu family kings. Its Naxi name Boa-shi means "Pumi death", possibly a reference to a battle against the Pumi, the original inhabitants of these lands. As Baisha was the ancestral home and first capital of the Mu Kings, their most important palaces and temples were built there, as the magnificent Dabaoji Temple with its unique frescoes, and the Beiyue Temple, the oldest temple in Lijiang, where Sanduo, the protector god of the Naxi, is worshipped (Yang 1999: 21). As the ritual center Baisha was the home where more and the most important Dongbas lived, the cultural center of the Naxi culture, and the place where their main artistic and musical traditions were created and preserved.

Villages and valleys in these central plains are protected by the magnificent Jade Dragon Snow Mountain, the southern permanent glacier in the northern hemisphere, whose 18 main peaks conform a wonderful labyrinth of rugged peaks, alpine meadows, glacial lakes and primeval forests, where an astonishingly rich variety of vegetal species are preserved. Over half of the 13.000 kinds of plants native to Yunnan can be found on the primeval forests of this mountain, as well as more than 400 types of rare trees. In spring the mountain is a sea of multicolor flowers, with azaleas, wild camellias, orchids, gentians, lilies and peonies blooming everywhere. Dragon Jade Mountain is also a paradise for many species of rare and precious animals living in its different climatic zones (Zhang and He 2005: 32- 33).

Jade Dragon Snow Mountain is a sacred mountain for the Naxi. In a clear day, it can be seen from most of the Naxi territories, which could be considered to lie around it. Its mountain god, Sanduo, is the most important of the nature gods worshipped by the Naxi and the protector of the Naxi kings. The exaltation of this deity by the Naxi kings was part of their strategy to set themselves in a central position, as the Chinese emperor in his domains. Jade Dragon Mountain is also a holy place of love for the Naxi and the gate to an imaginary paradise to those who committed love suicide. In the past it was the favorite place chose by Naxi young lovers that wanted to put an end to their lives. To get rid of the shackle of arranged marriage and feudal ethics they went to the snow mountain and sacrificed their young lives for ideal love, believing that they would immediately enter to an unrivalled clean and beautiful domain: The Third Yulong Kingdom, where "as legends say, live a couple of lovers, riding red tiger and white deer, whistling and blowing bamboo flute, leading a colony of birds and animals flying in clouds and winds, calling for the lovers in the secular world to fulfill their dream of love" (Yang 1999).

Though the Naxi in these central areas have been deeply influenced by Chinese culture, there are still many places where the traditions have been preserved, usually due to the merit of Dongba families, whose ceremonies and sacred scriptures are used in praying to their gods, funerals, spirit exorcisms and divination.

2. Baidi: the center of Dongba tradition

Across the Yangtze River, officially belonging to Deqin Tibetan Autonomous Prefecture, there is a cluster of Naxi villages usually known as Baidi or Baishuitai. Baidi and specially the famous white terraces known as Baishuitai are the sacred place of the Dongba, where new couples, unmarried girls and women who have no sons pray for descendants (Goodman 1997: 83). According to their legends both the founder of the Dongba religion Dongba Shiluo, and his main disciple Aming Shiluo, meditated for long time in one of the caves near the village. No Dongba priest is considered to be able to reach their highest levels if he has not studied in Baidi, under the guidance of the great Dongbas whose tradition has been kept uninterrupted here. The 20.000 Naxi living there belong to two branches: the Rerke and the Naheng. While the Naheng are culturally related to the Lijiang Naxi, being usually considered the purest of their race, the Rerke living in the most isolated places preserve a folk culture with unique flavor and a language that is not understood by other Naxi populations. These villages, difficult to access until the 20th century, are considered the cradle of Dongba culture and the place where their traditional religion was nurtured and preserved uncontaminated by foreign influences. Joseph Rock considers that: "The most primitive type of Naxi, undisturbed since they first settled many centuries ago, dwell in this region. Here they follow their old religious customs, which is a mixture of shamanism and the pre-Buddhistic Bon religion of Tibet. There are neither lamas nor lama temples as in the Lijiang district, nor are there any Chinese temples, for no Chinese live here. An interesting feature is the total absence of graves in Baidi, for here the Naxi still follow their traditional custom of cremating their dead. They take no medicines of any kind, but rely solely on their sorcerers to exorcize the demons of disease" (1946: 250). Baidi people dress, build their houses and marry following traditions already disappeared around Lijiang. They have retained also the original faith, Dongbas still play an active role in their society, and old rituals abandoned elsewhere continue to be performed here. Traditional festivals and dances are performed in Baidi with a special local flavor. The women wear a different kind of cape -a rectangular woven cloth, one metre by two metres, of wool or cotton, in no particular style or colour. They also wear a sheepskin of about the same size (He Shangli 2000: 32, 66; Goodman 1997: 83).

3. The territories in the west to the Mekong River: Ludian, Tacheng, Weixi, Yezhi.

The conquering impetus of the Mu kings led the Naxi expansion along the bank of the Yangtze River to Shigu (lit. Stone Drum), where the river changes its southward course and makes its first bend; a strategic point because it is the place more convenient to cross the powerful river. In Shigu a decisive battle was fought and won against the local Tibetans in 1561. This was also the point chosen by the Red Army to cross the river in 1949. Further to the west are the Naxi townships of Ludian, Judian and Tacheng, and even further in the Mekong basin some Naxi settlements up to Yezhi, ruled until the 1940s by a Naxi *tusi*. In this area the Naxi culture experienced almost imperceptible changes that gradually transformed some of their main characteristics, with language, writing, customs and ceremonies clearly differentiated. Among them the Malimasha living near Weixi, developed a writing system with special characteristics, and the Lulu living in Tacheng show differences in language, marriage and funerary rituals. Some writers consider that the Lulu are the product of the blending of Lisu and Naxi populations, their inclusion in the Naxi nationality being more related with administrative than cultural reasons.

4. The northern territories: Fengke, Baoshan.

North of Lijiang, on the loop of the Yangtze River, villages lying around Mingyin, Fengke and Baoshan are characterized as strongholds of traditional Naxi culture. There, a mountain terrain not suitable for wet rice agriculture and difficult communications were an insurmountable barrier to Chinese influence. In the mountain villages Naxi traditional culture, rituals and customs have many local features, with production, ritual cycle, and main ceremonies with a unique flavour. Their sexual relations follow patterns that could be considered halfway between the freest mother-oriented society of the Moso and the male-dominated one of Lijiang. The northern communities, known as Nari, due to their frequent relations with the Moso, have adopted many of their cultural characteristics. Some inhabitants of this area are known as Zherkhin by the Lijiang Naxi, or inhabitants of the *zherdu* or hot lands. Zher also means fear; they are so called because they

27

Place names in Naxi geography, from left to right. Dayan, the old city of Lijiang, Eya, Baidi (the mule image only for sound), Baoshan stone village, Shigu (laba in Naxi, la sounds as "tiger"), Ludian, Baisha, with palaces, Jade Dragon Snow Mountain, River of Golden Sands, and Beijing, the land of the emperor.

are sensitive to the cold uplands and are afraid to stay at the higher elevations. To call a man Zherkhin is not complimentary as the people of the lowlands are considered stupid (Rock 1972: 803).

5. Isolated communities of Eya

According to Naxi legends some 500 years ago the Mu king sent some of his generals to hunt and live in the remote Eya Township. During some time Eya people kept contact with Lijiang, sending their annual taxes to the kings. Political upheavals in the region put Eya under the rule of the big lamas of the Muli Kingdom. During hundreds of years Eya's Naxi have been completely isolated from the mainstream of their culture, preserving customs and traditions already disappeared elsewhere. Even today, the difficulty to access these lands, surrounded by powerful rivers and lofty mountains, keep the Naxi population there as a living museum of their ancestral culture. Eya Township is divided in 28 villages. Of the 5.000

people living there, 3.000 are Naxi, (He Shangli 2000: 76) most of them of the Rerke or Naheng branches, the rest are Tibetan and Pumi. Eya's Naxi culture is unique in its main features: houses, dress and social relations, are quite original. Most of the sexual arrangements found in neighbouring peoples have been reported in Eya, with polyandrous and polygynous marriages, marrying brothers or sisters or not related males or females, sexual freedom, lack of discrimination towards children born out of the marriage, etc. Festivals are also different in Eya, celebrated with completely different aims and rituals than in other Naxi areas.

Language

In the Naxi language we find reflected also the border character of this people and their incorporation of foreign elements; it belongs to the Sino-Tibetan language family, Tibeto-Burman branch, but it is considered as a transition language between the Qiangic and Burman languages, with some Loloish influences. Other Loloish (or Yi) languages are spoken by peoples living near the Naxi, as the Yi, Lisu, etc. Even today it is possible to find many cultural similarities between the Naxi and the peoples speaking Loloish languages. Naxi language has four tones, 31 consonants and 21 vowels. The initial consonant of the speech sound is divided into voiced and voiceless consonants, and its voiced initial consonants into pure voiced consonants and nasals ones. Most of the vowels are simple, the compound vowels used mainly in Chinese borrowed words. Syllables are usually composed of consonants and vowels and only a few of only vowels.

Monosyllabic roots take priority in Naxi language. The word order in the elementary sentence is subject –object – predicate, with nouns, verbs and pronouns placed before the key words, and adjectives after them (Xu 2003: 26-7).

Traditionally Naxi language has been divided into two main dialects: Eastern and Western, each in turn with three local speeches. In the usual fuss created by the blending of politics and linguistics, the Western dialect is the language spoken by the Naxi proper; its three main local variations reflect their past history, presenting only slight differences. The talk of Lijiang City is considered the "Standard Naxi", mainly spoken in Lijiang city and the neighboring villages (Baisha, Shuge, Daogu, etc) that constitute the heart of the Naxi culture, is spoken by around 30.000 persons. People living in the areas west of Lijiang, occupied by the Naxi after their conquest in the Ming Dynasty, speak the Lijiang variety, altogether about 100.000 people. "This area largely corresponds with the territory controlled by the feudal lords of Lijiang… The relative homogeneity of Naxi dialects is due to historical causes. The centralization of power in Lijiang created a degree of linguistic convergence, and the enforcement of conscription presumably played a role in leveling dialect differences" (Michaud 2011). The Baoshan talk is spoken by the communities living north of Lijiang, in the Yangtze loop. The Eastern dialect would correspond to the languages spoken by the Moso minority and related peoples. "They are so diverse that it appears more adequate to refer to them as distinct languages, rather that as dialects of a single language" (Michaud 2011: 3). Though a common origin of both dialects could be perceived, their differences make them mutually unintelligible

30

nowadays. Of the three local varieties of the Eastern dialect, the Yongning one is spoken by the Moso in Yongning and Yanyuan, who call themselves Na, and by the Malimasha Naxi near Weixi. The Beiquba variety is spoken near Yongshen County by people who call themselves Naheng, and the Guabie variety by people who call themselves Naru (He and He 1988; He and Jiang 1985). Other Naxi branches as the Rerke of Baidi and Eya, the Lare of Eya, the Lulu of Tacheng and Ludian, have not been sufficiently studied as to adscript their languages to one of the existing dialects (Guo and He 1994).

Dongba pictographic script

The Naxi use a pictographic script commonly called Dongba script, because it is primarily utilized by the Dongba priests when they carry out their ceremonies, rituals and exorcisms. This script, with about 1.400 individual pictographs, is the only pictographic language still in use in the world. It consists of two kinds of characters: Pictographic characters, stylized drawings of men, animals, plants, natural elements and cultural objects, and ideographic ones, which function as verbs or express abstract ideas. Besides, Dongba pictographs can be employed by their phonetic value, and can be used as mnemonic tools, as in the narration of myths and legends, when a single pictogram can point to a long history or tale. Dongba pictographs have three dimensions: a semantic one, a phonetic one and an allegoric one (Zamblera). The multiple meanings and functions of the pictographs make it possible to understand its actual meaning only in relation with a particular context. As the main ethnic marker of the Naxi, the pictographic script was used all over their territory in a rather anarchical way, with identical symbols showing local or even personal variations (Rock 1963: 331). Dongba writing is a performative writing, a sacred text that has for the Dongba priest the power to give birth to the concepts it represents.

The persistence of the Dongba spiritual tradition for over more than eight centuries has created a staggering number of Dongba Scriptures, possibly more than 50.000 volumes of sacred writings. These texts describe virtually every aspect of Naxi religion and culture, history, folklore, music, dance, medicine, and of course, their myths and legends. This amazing development of Dongba literature is due to the fact that when a Dongba priest performs a ceremony, he needs to narrate the origin of every spirit or sacred object that is summoned. The love of the Naxi for their culture is shown in the care with which these pictographs were preserved in the more remote areas. Though in the 20th century it was thought that the Dongba script was doomed to disappear, nowadays the Dongba religion and the rituals associated with it are actively encouraged and taught to the younger generation. The revitalization of the Dongba tradition, the hallmark of Naxi culture, make their pictographic script, not only saved from near oblivion, but thrive, as it is actively studied ad promoted by a new generation of young Dongbas.

The construction of the Dongba pictograms is amazing. Most of them are derived from about a hundred basic drawings. For instance, a person is represented by the basic lines of his shape. A person belonging to one of the ethnic groups who live in their vicinity: Tibetan, Chinese, Bai, Yi,

Lisu or Pumi, would be written stressing some of his ethnic characteristics.

From left to right, the pictograms to write: person, Naxi, Pumi, Yi, Lisu, Bai, and Tibetan. The first is the pictograph of a person, an outline of his head, arms, body and legs. In the Naxi pictograph the "na" black character in their name is denoted in various ways, the Pumi are characterized for the long hair that grows from their heads, the Bai emphasizes the original headdress of the Bai women near Lijiang, The Tibetan are distinguished by the long braid of the Tibetan women (He Baolin 2007).

If they want to express some of the person's activities, the part of the body affected is emphasized: the mouth, hand, leg, etc. Below are shown some common activities of human beings as seen in the Dongba script. The meaning is, from left to right: to stand, with the feet added to the person drawing, to sit dawn, with the skirt covering the legs, to jump, moving arms and legs, to dance, and to walk along a stretch of land (Zhao 1998).

In the same way most of the pictograms related to animals, birds or trees share their common characteristics, as do some of the related to their gods and spirits. Though the Dongba script seems to be very simple and easy to learn, as it would be easy to memorize the basic pictographs without great difficulty, the reality is different.

In the above picture we see the title of a Dongba ceremony extracted from a book of the leading specialist of Naxi culture, Joseph F. Rock. The manuscript is called "To relate the history of Do-sau-ngo-t'u". The reading of this title is as follows:

"The first upper symbol is an ideogram and denotes the action of seeing = (do), the second is read ssaw = breath; both are used phonetically in the name of the Naxi whose history is counted. The syllables ngo= I and t'u =a trough which would be used

34

ordinarily for the two other phonetics in the name are not written. Instead we have the figure of a man wearing a large hat, such as the Tibetan nomads still wear in the grasslands of the northeastern Tibet, especially in the region of the headwaters of the Yellow River. The last read dzo to record, to relate; dso ba means to speak about a man (behind his back), as well as to speak for a man" (Rock 1952: 307).

From this example we can see that the Dongba script, though simple in its conception, grew to become a writing system really complex. The phonetic use of the pictograms, and the omission of those pictographs supposed to be known by the Dongba priests, make this sacred language almost impossible to read to the non initiated. As this script was not used for administration or literature, but only for ritual and religious activities, and the only people who could read it were the Dongba priests that had been trained in their religious traditions, their ceremonies, and the use of the sacred books, the pictographs became in their hands a mnemonic device intended not as a narrative, but as a prompt towards a fuller, more embellished and undoubtedly personalized telling of the stories pertaining to the rituals. For any student of Naxi culture the key to be able to read their religious texts in not only to know the meaning of the 1.400 pictographs, but also a good knowledge of the Naxi spoken language that will allow to know which pictographs are used phonetically, indicating sound rather than meaning (Hsu 1998: 17).

To have an idea of the aspect of a Dongba manuscript, we can look at the above fragment of "The War between Dong and Shu", one of the most important myths in the Naxi. One page is divided in three rows, and each row in several cells containing the basic units of information, sometimes a verse of a sacred reading. Its first paragraph is translated into Chinese by the Naxi scholar He Limin: "In the old times, when the sky and the earth had not still been formed, the sun and moon had still not been created, the stars had still not arisen (end of the first cell), mountains and ravines had not still been formed, trees and stones had not still arisen..." (Office: 1989).

Most of the elements of this narrative can be easily found in the first line of the script: heaven, earth, sun, moon, stars, mountains, trees and stones, and near them the symbols for negation. The tiger at left, suggests the old times, the beginning of time, as some myths narrate that the tiger created the world.

The Naxi don't think it is enough to posses the most original writing system on the planet. They still use among them another writing system, the Geba syllabic script; a phonetic form of writing generally employed for spells (where the sound alone was important), considered the little brother of the Dongba script, although they possibly have the same antiquity. In the several hundred books extant written in Geba script, 686 characters have been identified. The origins of these two kinds of scripts are still the subject of a hot discussion among the academics, but it is possible to see in the Geba a blending of Dongba pictographs, Chinese characters and Yi syllabic script, as the samples below suggest.

Among the Naxi there are still two others types of writing: The Rerke characters used in Eya and Baidi, and the Masha writing. Among the Rerke living in Eya township after the death of a person, it should be a Rerke Dongba who conducts the funeral in the Rerke dialect. Because of that they have 35 sacred books written in a pictographic script that shows some interesting differences with the Dongba script. Here we show a sample of their writing.

Nevertheless, the Masha writing system demonstrates best the Naxi people's love and appreciation of culture, because it was developed by a community of scarcely 100 families that arrived 200 years ago to the region of Weixi, from Dongba characters that a shaman taught them.

The Shaba shamans of the Ersu people that live in the south of Sichuan Province use in their religious ceremonies a pictographic script consisting of 200 pictographs. The structure and meaning of these pictographs shows similarities with the Dongba script, with which it is possibly related. Below there is a sample of the Ersu script, as shown in Sun Hongkai *The Ersu Shaba pictographic writing* (2009).

Origin of Naxi scripts

There are not only different theories about the origin of the Dongba characters, but even different classifications of these theories. Following He Limin (2003) we could summarize them in three groups: the first is sustained by these scholars that believe, with J.F. Rock at their head, that the pictographs were invented around Lijiang. Their main argument is that most of the fauna and flora described in the pictographs can be found in this area; the second group follows

Li Lincan in the belief that the pictographs were created around the Wulianghe River, north of Lijiang, as the pictograph for water shows a river flowing from north to south; the third group relate the origin of the Dongba script with wood paintings discovered in Dunhuang, possibly made by the ancestors of the Qiang. Li Jingsheng (2003), one of the most ardent defenders of this last theory has studied old systems of signs used in the border between Gansu and Qinghai provinces, in what could be the ancestral home of the Qiang forefathers of the Naxi, discovering that both the signs used in pottery unearthed in Qinghai province as well as in wooden slabs hidden in the Dunhuang grottoes, show striking similarity with the Dongba pictographs. Mr. Li considers that the creation of the Dongba pictographs could have been a long process that began when the Naxi still lived far from their present home; the presence of the simpler pictographic scripts of the Ersu and the Malimasha (who migrated from Muli to Weixi) would reinforce his evolutionary theory. His arguments seem too weak to demonstrate that the creation of the Dongba script was an evolutionary process developed along centuries, but they provide information that suggests that systems of signs were used by the Qiang and peoples related to them from immemorial times in religious contexts, and that some of them could have been used with the same meaning all this time. His discovery fits perfectly also with what is known of the sacred art of the Naxi, specially the wooden slabs and figurines used in some of their ceremonies.

In the 1990s at least 10 sites were discovered along the banks of the River of Golden Sands containing rock paintings depicting animal and human figures, "shown in a range of poses, from standardized profiles to highly innovative and creative position… running, standing, climbing, leaping –either on their own or as part of a group", and signs of difficult classification that are unlike any other known body of rock art in China (Tacon et al 2010). Most of these paintings are found between the first and second winding of the River, an area where the Dongba religion was well developed and preserved. A study of these rock paintings shows that some of them have a similarity with the Dongba pictographs, which were originally based also in nature designs. While these paintings fit well with the Naxi name for their own script: "Paint on rocks and trees", the long difference in time, and cultural and social development between the authors of the rock art and the Naxi people, make it difficult to establish a connection between them, though the rock art could have inspired the first Dongba pictographs (He Limin 2003).

There is an interesting debate about the antiquity of the Dongba and Geba scripts. Most of the Chinese scholars, following the history of Chinese characters, whose most primitive forms were also pictographic, consider that the Dongba pictographs must have precede the Geba syllabic script. Among the Western researchers there is not a unanimous opinion. While Jackson and others think that their origin is quite recent, attributing it an age of about 300 years, Christine Mathieu, relying in the similarity between the Geba and the syllabic script used among the Yi, suggests that the Geba syllabic script could have arrived to Lijiang "during Nanzhao times and probably earlier." This early relation between Naxi and Yi script could contribute to explain the origin of that part of the Dongba ritual that antedate the Bon influences, as well as the correspondence between some Dongba and Yi ceremonies (Mathieu 2003: 171). Being difficult to explain why the Naxi invented a new pictographic script if they were already using a syllabic one, she stresses the importance of the rock art tradition that flourished in the area before the Naxi conquest, suggesting that the Naxi chose to write in pictures because pictures had a sacredness of their own to the people they conquered, a sacredness already established in rock art, maybe related with shamanistic traditions (Mathieu 2003: 187 to 219). Chinese and Western attempts to relate the Dongba pictographs with the rock art discovered in the banks of the River of Golden Sands must be considered only conjectural, as the first international research expedition has been unable to determine its age and the nature of its possible authors. The almost inaccessible location of some of the most interesting samples of the rock art, and its artistic similitude with rock art of Western Europe and Africa thousands of years old, make even more difficult to establish a connection with the much later Dongba pictographs.

Another evolutionary theory related to the technological development of the Dongba pictograms proposes that "Originally, these characters were carved on stones. When people invented iron tools and were able to make wooden slaps, they were written on wooden slaps. Later the scriptures were also written on tree's bark and animals' skin. At last Naxi people learned to make paper, and were painted on paper" (He and He 1999: 19).

As to the time when the Dongba script began to be used, most of the scholars consider that they must have originated between the 11th to 13th centuries. Mathieu thinks that "There is reasonable evidence that the Dongbas were already writing pictographic manuscripts during the Mongol period or at least they were writing pictographic books at a period when Mongol influence was still dominant, as some pictographs could not have come into the Dongba's repertoire if the Naxi had not had significant contacts with the Mongols." Although the Dongba religion is heavily influenced by the Bon Tibetan tradition, their writing doesn't seem to have Tibetan influences, at least in its purely formal aspect. The absence of manuscripts in the region of Yongning and the Lugu Lake, suggests that the pictographs may have been invented in Lijiang, at a time when the Lijiang chiefs no longer had jurisdiction over Yongning –i.e. post 14th century (Mathieu 2003: 163-166).

CHAPTER 2

Echoes from the past:
Naxi
History

The Naxi nationality is the result of the blending of different races and peoples, including aboriginal populations of northwest Yunnan, waves of Qiang migrants, tribes of Tibetan stock, and individuals of Mongolian, Bai and Chinese origin. The formation of the Naxi ethnic group reflects the tensions, also presents in their religion and culture, inherent to frontier territories lying between some of the most powerful empires of Asia. A detailed research on their old culture could allow to recreate the original shape and the key characteristics of these past empires, as the Naxi, with an astonishing ability to integrate into their lives foreign influences, remain a repository of cultural forms and thoughts already disappeared elsewhere.

Archaeological discoveries show that the area around Lijiang was inhabited from 50-100.000 years ago, when the called Man of Lijiang, whose skull was discovered south of this city in 1964, lived there. Human presence could have been most or less continuous in the area, as more rests of Paleolithic settlements were discovered in subsequent years (Outlook

1999). While it is impossible to know the original culture of the antique inhabitants of the Lijiang region, the cultural artifacts left by them show some characteristics that can be traced to the present. Among them has paramount importance the rock-art in the banks of the Yangtze River, and the presence of stone coffins, which were placed on a hole carved on the earth, usually on an elevation near a confluence of two or three rivers, and of objects of stone, pottery and bronze, accompanying the dead (Guo and He 1994).

The Qiang tribes of Northwest China

With the name Qiang are designated groups of nomad herders that lived in Northwest China from ancient times. Their name is already found in the oracle bones of the Shang Dynasty (17th to 12th century BCE), usually referred to as enemies against whom bloody wars were fought. Waves of Qiang tribes moved south from the sources of the Yellow River, mixed with the aboriginals who lived in the northwest of Yunnan and west of Sichuan, and they gave birth to most of the ethnic groups speaking Tibeto-Burman languages nowadays. The forefathers of the Naxi are considered late Qiang migrants, heading south maybe as a result of the territorial conquests of the Qin that lead to the unification of China or to the ethnic conflicts that surged in the first years of the Han dynasty as consequence of the Chinese migrations to Qiang lands. Tribes of Qiang herders displaced by the Chinese expansion that migrated south along the Tibetan-Yi corridor in western Sichuan. It is possible that some of the main features of Naxi culture took shape during their migrations, as some

44

cultural and linguistic resemblances can be established with the ethnic groups now inhabiting the Tibetan-Yi corridor. The relation between the Dongba pictographs and those used by the Shuba shaman of the Ersu has been already noted. The leading scholar of Naxi culture Yang Fuquan (2009), has discovered a close relationship between the Naxi and the Namuji. Based in the relationship between them in history and ethnographies, he considers that the Namuji belong to the same family than the Naxi, finding similitudes in their religion, culture, folk literature and artistic works. Regarding their myths, religion and ceremonies, both Naxi and Namuji have illustrated scrolls to guide the souls of the dead, both perform the washing of the horse ceremony to take the souls out of the purgatory, both have a kind of priest devoted to formal rituals and other, usually female, dedicated to divination practices, and both share a myth of the recreation of human beings after the deluge and the celestial marriage of its only survivor, with the names of the main protagonists almost identical.

Qiang southward migrations must be considered a slow movement of tribes probably related by blood ties, with long stops in convenient lands, sometimes even for hundreds of years, and occasional departures when news of fertile lands or struggle with a difficult environment or unfriendly neighbours forced them to. Historical records suggest that there were several waves of Qiang migrations, some as early as 4.000 years ago. Along the centuries, people of later waves intermingled in Southwest China with those early arrived and with aboriginal populations, giving form to the ethnic groups nowadays present in the area. Qiang migrants could have arrived at the Lijiang region about 2000 years ago; it was the end of epic adventures in which a wide array of situations can have happened along a considerable lapse of time: From big tribes travelling together until they found a place for themselves, to lonely survivors or smaller bands that were welcomed by the original populations. There is no evidence to probe that the Qiang migrants overpowered the original populations; history and myth suggest that a wide range of interaction happened, nor excluding war and fighting.

History books mention that in the 3rd century of the Common Era the Moxie or Moxie Yi, possibly ancestors of the Naxi, were living in the region located to the east of their current position. He Shaoying (2001) considers that the Naxi nationality was formed by the merging of three ethnic groups: tribes of Qiang migrants merged with the Bailang Yi or Maoniu Yi (Yak Barbarians), living in South Sichuan, and with peoples of Qiang stock previously arrived, mainly Pu or Pumi.

Establishment in their present area

In the 6th and 7th centuries, the political development of northwest Yunnan led some chiefs to establish the first Naxi statelet of historical relevance: The Yuexi or Moxie zhao. At this time, the Naxi lived east of the Lijiang region, while Lijiang was occupied by the Pu ancestors of the present day Pumi nationality, well established in this region at least from the 5th century. These facts fit well with the information linguistics provide us. If the Pumi were early Qiang migrants and the Naxi later ones, the language of the Naxi must be closer to the Qiang language. But the fact that the Pumi language is closer to the Qiang suggests that they must have

46

been later migrants. The centuries' long stop of the Naxi east of Lijiang can explain their impregnation from Yi (Lolo) language and culture, and their late arrival to Lijiang.

Before entering Lijiang, the Naxi could have been led by sacred leaders, maybe shamans. Later chiefs of the Mu family were also considered invested with magic powers, as seen in the history of Maizhong, credited with the invention of the pictographic characters and with understanding the language of the birds. After embracing the Buddhist faith, the relation of the kings with their original religion was weaker. In different Dongba documents the social development of the Naxi could be revealed, from a time when they lived in caves as hunter-gatherers (maybe in their ancestral lands before starting their migrations), to the age when they were nomad herders with an economy based in the yak (their migrating years), and to the agricultural and trade settlements that are known in historical sources (Guo: 1991).

Though it seems that the Naxi chiefs took control of Lijiang as the vanguard of the powerful Nanzhao Kingdom, previous interaction between Naxi and Pumi must have been common. Some Naxi tribes were friendly received by the Pu, and some chiefs married Pu princesses and become chiefs through this marriage, as we read in the chronicles: "At that time a certain Xian-tao A-ku from Baisha was the chief of the barbarians. He saw signs of nobility on the face and the bearing of Yeh-yeh (the ancestor of the Naxi); he also noticed his calmness and imperturbability (retiring attitude) and marveled greatly in his heart. Thereupon he gave him his daughter in marriage" (Rock 1947: 73). These Pumi must have had a good knowledge of agriculture, as it is written in a Dongba manuscript: "Before the birds were, the trees have been born, before the Naxi had settled, the Pu were settled; where the Pu were settled it was unnecessary to look for food" (Rock 1947).

Myths, traditions and historical documents suggest that the rich plains around Lijiang and Baidi were the territory of the most powerful Pumi chiefs, and the military objective of their Naxi counterparts. It is possible that the decisive battle for the control of these fertile valleys were fought around present day Baisha, as its Naxi name Boa-shi means literally "Pumi death" (Rock: 1947). Myth and history also tell of peace and accommodation between the former inhabitants and the newly arrived migrants, and a transmission of the political power through the marriage with local princesses. Neither the Pumi nor the Naxi of these times had constructed a centralized political entity. War and peace, conflict and accommodation must be considered as part of the options of the ruling families of both peoples, and maybe of other peoples now unknown to us, in their political relations. Most of the information we have about Naxi history refers to the history of the Lijiang plains and the Naxi Mu family, not only because "Naxi history is "heroic history," a history that belongs to the most influential groups, especially the prominent Mu royal family" (Mathieu 2003: 33), but also because only the Mu family chiefs have the need to carefully relate the feats of their kings. Nevertheless, out of this heroic history registered in the official chronicles, people experienced their own history, a history that far from the war and violence that seem inherent to kingly histories could have been based in accommodation and cooperation between different peoples. It seems that in isolated areas as Baidi, where traditions tell of thousands of years of occupation of the lands,

48

the integration of Naxi migrants with aboriginal populations was a peaceful process that produced no discontinuity of the social life, maybe because the power was transmitted by the female side.

The Eastern Kingdom of Women

In a time characterized by the coexistence of tribes of different stocks in the present Naxi area, it seems that the bulk of the Naxi population could have lived enjoying matriarchal societies. Chinese Tang dynasty chronicles attest to the existence of the Women Kingdom of the East, that would be situated near present day Moso and Naxi territories.

Many authors have established a relationship between the Eastern Kingdom of Women and the Moso people of today. Based in the fact that the Moso and the Naxi were not still differentiated in those years, the relationship between the forefathers (mothers) of the Naxi and the Eastern Kingdom of Women could also be established. As Zamblera points out this kingdom do not need to be interpreted as a unified polity with defined boundaries, but as a social model that would include some matriarchal tribes.

Mathieu (2003) sees further traces of the existence of a matriarchal society in the incongruence of the Mu genealogies, which she discovered changed to fit a new patriarchal model, and in the transmission of power through royal princesses. We have shown that, out of the sinicized area around Lijiang, differences among the Moso and the Naxi are not so easily perceived, and even today, the Naxi with a freer love mores are called Moso by other Naxi (Ceinos 2011). It is possible that in

Naxi Helmet and armour from the Lijiang Museum of Dongba Culture

these years the mother line, emphasized in the first syllable of the name, was most important than the father line, expressed in the second, and the power of the group was symbolized by the power of its matriarch (Zamblera).

Nanzhao and Dali Kingdoms

In the sixth and seventh centuries the political development of Northwest Yunnan led to the establishment of several important chieftains (called *zhao*). As six of them were more powerful this time is called in the local histories as the Six Zhaos. In the 8th century Nanzhao Kingdom (the Kingdom of the South) become the most powerful; backed by the Chinese Tang Dynasty attacked and conquered the other kingdoms. In 738 A.D. the Naxi chief Pochung was defeated and murdered and the Moxie Zhao was absorbed by Nanzhao; its ruling class fled to north-central Yunnan and some regrouped themselves around Lijiang (Jackson 1979: 11). Once its control of

50

northwest Yunnan firmly held, the first Nanzhao king Piluoge started a series of victorious campaigns that gave him the control of Yunnan province, as well as portions of neighbouring countries and Chinese provinces. Later, at the end of the 8th century the Naxi were used to subjugate Judian district and incorporate it into Nanzhao through subjection to the Lijiang chiefs (Jackson 1979: 11).

As the prosperity of the Nanzhao Kingdom was based in the control of the trade routes that connected China, Tibet and India; Lijiang, the natural gate to Tibet, gained in relevance, playing an important role in the trade and political relations with the then powerful Tubo (Tibetan) Kingdom. As a battlefield in the Nanzhao-Tubo military conflicts and as a market place in peaceful times, the Lijiang area slowly evolved into one of the secondary centers of Northwest Yunnan. The government of Lijiang was awarded to the chiefs of the Yang family (called Ye in some chronicles). One of the first chiefs Yang Du-gu La-ju consolidated Nanzhao occupation when he married a princess of the La ruling clan, one of the most powerful aboriginal Pumi clans of the area (Mathieu 2003: 82). Between 751 and 902 Lijiang was under the political control of the Yang clan backed by Nanzhao (He and He 1999), a control continuously challenged by the La tribes of Pumi origin, backed by the Tibetans (Mathieu 2003: 386).

The fall of the Nanzhao Kingdom in 902 in a bloody palatial rebellion was accompanied in Lijiang with the loss of power of the Yang associated with them, and the falling apart of the tribal federation that had expanded across northwestern Yunnan under their control. The Pumi reconquered their lands, but in the Lijiang plains the position of the Yang was occupied by the Mou (or Mu) clan that controlled however a much smaller territory (Mathieu 2003: 85). The Mu, which may have been related in the maternal side with the Yang family, became the leaders of a "system of tribal confederation based on alternative matrilateral alliances where the high-status group (the chief's group) was the wife-taking group, and where one specific clan – the La – appears to have held a privileged position" (Mathieu 2003: 77). The word "La" means tiger in the languages of the Naxi, Moso, Yi and Pumi, whilst all these peoples as well as the Chinese, the Qiang and the Tibetans consider the tiger a symbol of kingship. It is quite possible that the La was the "royal" lineage among local tribes, or alternatively, that "La" was the totemic title given to the ruling clan. The La clan held an important role in the political movements of these lands during centuries, even millennia, as their chiefs ruled Zuosou (in the Sichuan border of Lugu Lake) semi-independently until the 20th century (Mathieu 2003: 81).

These facts show that "dynastic change was ritually legitimized through the marriage of the conqueror to a local princess, usually the chief's or king's daughter, or even his widow. Because "the marriage of the king's daughter implies the transfer of original ancestral souls to her husband so that the ancestor of the defeated king became the conqueror's; marriages mythologically enshrined in stories of heavenly princesses marrying earthly men" (Mathieu 2003: 196- 7). In that way the Mu, considered heirs of both the Yang and La chiefs, were allowed to reunite other tribes under their rule. The transmission of the political power through the women of the ruling family is consistent with the information provided by Chinese legends and historical records that describe the prominent role of the women in southwest China local societies and even, in some instances, their monopoly of the political power.

With the ascent to power of the Mu family the Naxi underwent marked changes, as agriculture replaced livestock breeding as the main occupation of the people and settlements become larger and more stable, especially in the rich plains between Baisha and Lijiang. As the Mu power increased they borrowed concepts of sacred kingship from the Tibetan and Chinese traditions. In Tibet, the Mu signifies a heavenly lineage and the heavenly rope which allows the kings to travel between heaven and earth, in Chinese Mu means tree, a tree that in the Dongba cosmology acquired a mythical dimension: The tree that stands on top of the cosmic mountain, the *axis mundi*, the pillar between heaven and earth (Mathieu 2003: 110).

Allied with the Mongols of Kublai Khan

The arrival of Kublai Khan in 1253 at the head of his army marks a turning point in the history of Yunnan. The object of his invasion was to capture Dali, the capital of Nanzhao, and in a clip movement attack the Song Dynasty both from the north and the south. The Mongol army crossed the Yangtze River using skin-made bags inflated with air, and made a three-pronged attack on Lijiang. At Fengke the Naxi king A Liang welcomed the powerful Kublai Khan, helping him to subjugate various tribes, and guiding his army all the way to conquer Dali. Following the Mongol custom of exterminating those who opposed them and reward those who help them, A Liang received an official appointment to govern as a *tusi* (local chief) the territories included in the newly established Lijiang Prefecture, with the duty to pay tribute to the royal court and to send soldiers to assist the emperor in

Stone Drum in Shigu

times of war. This appointment was later handed down to his successors, as after him all the Naxi *tusi* belonged to his family, and were considered hereditary kings of Lijiang. His dynastic line kept the power until the administrative reforms of 1721, being considered invested of ritual and social prestige until 1949 (Jackson 1979: 12; Zhang 2000).

Naxi chronicles written during the Ming dynasty, established after the Mongols were defeated, however, in an effort to distance the Naxi chiefs from the Mongol empire and to show an early allegiance to the Chinese side, state that the Naxi refused to submit to Kublai Khan and were subsequently conquered. As histories were written centuries later and adapted to suit present political interests, it seems that some of the Naxi tribes welcomed the army of Kublai Khan, while others tried to resist it, because we know for the Mu chronicle that "during the reign of A Zhong (the father of A Liang) the different clans of the Naxi were divided in several small states that competed with each other for supreme power." One of the main alliances of tribes was headed by A Liang, that later unified under him the tribes loyal to the Mongols and with their support, pursued and vanquished the resistant. It is possible that alliances of small tribes under the guidance of several big chiefs were already underway from the time of A Zhong, as the chronicles credit him with this task. However, the contradictory notices about the arrival of the Mongol army to Naxi lands and the praise of A Liang for subjugating various tribes suggest that it was during A Liang rule, and with Mongol support, that the Naxi became a centralized polity. In fact, there are notices that state that while certain Naxi chiefs collaborated with Kublai Khan, others resisted for twenty years, until 1273, when most of the Naxi and Lolo tribes of the area surrendered. Joseph Rock tried to solve these contradictory records suggesting that after a first defeat on the hands of the Mongols, the Naxi turned to allegiance in all sincerity (1947: 60). We must keep in mind that the main objective of the Mongol army was not to subdue the mountain tribes of northwest Yunnan but the powerful Dali Kingdom and eventually the whole Chinese empire.

A Liang was the descendant in third generation of

Generals and soldiers in Dongba pictographs, from left to right: general, with a flag to lead the soldiers; a hero, with a special headdress; a soldier, with a weapon at hand; and an enemy, with weapon and a strange headdress.

Yekunian, which according to the legends arrived floating on a wood log over the Yangtze River and married a local princess. Later his son was chosen as his successor, maybe after marry one more local princess. His grandson Nian-pao A Zhong is credited with understanding Chinese characters, the invention of the Dongba writing and with the ability of understanding the language of birds. The two ancestors of A Liang seem to have possessed shamanistic powers; powers that could have helped them to rule over local populations. To descend the Yangtze River on a log is a heroic and symbolic portent, as it is to understand the language of birds[7]. The genealogy of A Liang was later traced back to mythical times to relate the Mu family

---

[7] "The shamans' secret language is an imitation of animal cries, or the sounds of birds. To know bird language enables one to understand all Nature's secrets, and to prophesy (Stutley 2002: 17).

with the first post-flood ancestor Congrenlien, and through his wife, Cunhongbaobai, to the same God of Heaven Zilao Apu. With the submission of the Dali Kingdom to the Mongol army in 1253, the region started a gradual integration into the Chinese Empire. Members of Kublai Khan's army settled in the region as the aristocracy of both the present-day Naxi and Moso, which claim a Mongol connection and even a direct line of descent from Mongol high officials (Hsu: 1998).

The Naxi kings in the Ming dynasty

In 1368 Chinese rebels defeated the last Mongol emperor of the Yuan dynasty and established the Ming dynasty. The new dynasty waited nearly 20 years before trying to take control of Yunnan province. In 1382 Emperor Hongwu sent an army to conquer Yunnan; they fought a bloody campaign that faced not only the resistance of the last Mongols, but of the fiery independent aboriginal tribes of Yunnan, that were ruthlessly suppressed. Chronicles record that in the eastern part of Yunnan 30,000 heads were cut off, and of 200,000 insurgents who attacked Kunming, 60,000 were decapitated (Rock 1947: 10). Thousands of aborigines were killed in minor battles, and a rosary of forts and fortified villages were built along the battle line to ensure that the peace so expensively gained, was kept. Amid this hostile environment, the chief of the Naxi, Mu De, was one of the first local leaders who swore allegiance to the new dynasty. He helped the Chinese general Fu Youde to wipe out the Mongol resistance, and to fight some important battles that secured him the control of the territory.

When King Mu De went to Nanjing to give in person the Naxi tribute to the Emperor Hongwu, the emperor was so pleased that he bestowed the surname Mu (tree) upon him and confirmed his family's position. This title was transmitted to his heirs by patrilineal line, agglutinating around his power in Lijiang the Naxi tribes. In this way, although a Chinese administration began to take shape in the area, Chinese rule was nominal only; real power remained in the hands of the native chiefs (Rock 1947: 63). The reason behind the emperors will to grant this special position to native leaders (*tusi*) is explained in the introductory paragraphs of the 1516 Mu family chronicle:

"Owing to bad communications and natural barriers, this land is separated far from the imperial rule. This it is advisable to make the native leader of this people their ruler. He is given an official seal by the emperor and also the hereditary right to control the land and its people. Such privileges are not accorded simply as a reward for merit acquired, but form part of a special policy of the government applied to suit the circumstances of the people. This means that their manners and customs are so different from ours, that the Emperor is obliged to allow the native rulers to maintain their hereditary right" (Rock 1947: 67).

Though the Naxi enjoyed native autonomy the Mu chiefs were vassals of the Chinese emperors, and one of the most trustworthy allies of the imperial court in Yunnan, with military service playing a crucial role in their contribution to the empire, a contribution that should not be underestimated.

Successive Mu kings not only kept at bay the mountain peoples living beyond their lands, but carried on a conquering campaign that, mountain after mountain, village after village, moved the Chinese border further to the west, pushing further the Tibetan border and bringing the local tribal peoples under imperial rule. Besides, Naxi troops were deployed in the Ming armies campaigning against Eryuan to the south and Yongsheng to the east, and Naxi soldiers acquired fame in the expeditions to pacify non Chinese peoples like the Dai of southwestern Yunnan, the Lisu of the Nu River and the Xifan tribes of southwestern Sichuan (Goodman 1997: 23). To guard China's borders and find the resources to pay yearly tribute to the court, the Mu engaged in a perpetual conquest, and as they went about pacifying, unifying, taxing, and conscripting, they expanded their dominion over a large territory (Mathieu 2003: 35). The history of Lijiang is intimately connected with its ruling chiefs. The Mu family chronicles reflect their war-like character, and merit them with major contributions to the Chinese empire in the constant extension of their west frontier. Wars, attacks, murder of enemies, are the main facts to be remarked of each of the reigning kings (Rock 1947: 46).

In 1499 the Naxi captured Zhongdian. In later years, they marched up to the Lancang River, beyond Deqin, and founded garrisons at selected points, where Naxi villages still exist. The greatest victory of the Naxi troops was Mu Gao's annihilation of a powerful Tibetan army at Shigu in 1561. In 1681 Mu Yao scored a significant victory over the Tibetans thanks to his use of Lisu auxiliaries (Zhang and He 26). Naxi kings' records of their war activities, periodically sent to the imperial authorities to see their hereditary titles confirmed, are a detailed exposition of their slow expansion. Every single village conquered is carefully noted. The destruction carried, the number of enemies killed, the submission of local chiefs, the imposition of a tribute, the number of labouring men obtained for corvee, the punishment of rebels and Tibetans, the number of heads chopped off, and the establishment of garrisoned villages (Mathieu 2003: 34, 193). All the military feats performed to the major glory of the Chinese Empire are in this way registered, remembering to the imperial administration the benefit of having so faithful an ally in these faraway lands. Chronicles confirm that the Lijiang chiefs gathered their people unto their persons throughout a long and murderous battle, and that it took them the better part of two centuries (1400-1600) to secure the mountain territories and bring the various hill tribes under the ritual, fiscal and military control of Lijiang. With the region of Zhongdian and Baidi coming under control of the Mu kings at the end of the 16th century, the long and bloody struggle that began 200 years ago was officially ended.

In the Mu continuous conquest of new territories the Dongba priests carried on a ritual role that completed the military expansion, integrating the new lands into the spiritual domain of the kings. Naxi religion reflects a military ethos, a mythology concerned with the acquisition of spiritual power that accompanies territorial transfer, and the chronicles, crucial to the reconstruction of the history of the region, "become quite intelligible when they are read from the perspective of Naxi magic and symbolism" (Mathieu 2003: 198). Because when the conquest takes place in the wild tribal frontiers where there are no kings and therefore, no king's daughters to be married, the spirits of the land cannot be appropriated, but must be suppressed and exorcized (Mathieu 2003: 194-6). Maybe this is the first instance of human (Naxi) encroachment of Shu or other territorial spirit's domains, and also the first instance of the Dongba acting as a mediator between humans and nature. The conquest and colonization of new territories required that the souls of the previous occupants' dead ancestors, warriors and shamans, the guardian spirits of their sacred sites, be pacified and ritually appropriated by the conqueror. This ritual adjustment could have been provided by the Shu nature cults that annually renovated the Naxi right to enjoy the benefits of the lands (Mathieu 2003: 198-201).

The Mu kings were at the center of a web of local relations that provided them with an exceptional position in regional politics. Relations forged through matrimonial alliances with neighbouring *tusi*, cultural links with the Tibetan *karmapa* lamas, shown in the Mu kings donation of money to the publishing of their *kangur* canon, and their patronage of Buddhist and Lamaist temples in areas as far as Jizu Mountain, east of Dali. The Mu kings encouraged the development of an economy not based only in agricultural production. Long distance trade, mining of silver in the mountains and of gold in the rivers and valleys, gathering of medicinal and aphrodisiacal products from the forest, and the raising of horses and cattle were also important economic activities, which provided them with personal wealth and means to pay the yearly tribute owed to the imperial court (Mathieu 2003: 34). Under their rule Lijiang achieved a period of great affluence characterized by a stable society, prosperous economy, increasing financial resources, and cultural development. The manners and customs of the ruling elite slowly changed to fit local conceptions of

Chinese culture. Buddhist temples and Chinese style schools were established in Lijiang after 1418. Chinese cultural, technical and artistic influences were constant. The climax was reached when Mu De built a royal palace designed to imitate the Forbidden City in Beijing.

The development of agricultural techniques brought an enrichment of the society and a bigger social division. The Mu family was at the top of the social ladder. The king owned a great deal of land. According to the records compiled in 1743, the Mu held hereditary estates of about 5,000 acres. In addition, they controlled another 2,500 acres of cultivated fields and, with those, 500 households (2340 people) (Mathieu 2003: 34). Under the king were village headmen; often related to the ruling families in the capital, of which two levels existed, depending of the size of the village. The kings and nobles dressed in Chinese fashion and followed the Chinese marriage and funeral customs, while the commoners wore tribal clothes, were ignorant of Chinese, practiced a form of shamanism, cremated their dead, married whom they pleased, and presumably had matrilineal descent (Jackson 1979: 19, 37). The transformation of Naxi society changed in the minds of the aristocratic elite a sense of ethnic conscience for a new one of class conscience that aligned them with the Chinese elites; a policy purposely followed from the Chinese court, aimed to firmly establish their suzerainty over these lands, that perfectly combined the rigour in the control of the taxes and tributes due, with a generosity in providing imperial gifts and outward signs of rank and nobility (Bacot 1913: 139).

Chinese rule under Manchu emperors

High status officials under the Qing administration in Dongba pictographs, from left to right: emperor, king, counselor, marshall, and elder.

To strengthen imperial control of the borders of China and allow the central government a direct rule of these territories, Emperor Yongzheng (1723-1735) developed a policy of replacing native officials with imperial-appointed magistrates, known as *gaituguiliu* or "replacing the local and reverting to the mainstream." The first step of this policy was to abolish the *tusi* system, replacing the native chiefs with officials or magistrates dispatched from the central court. The *gaituguiliu* policy responded to the need of the Qing government of ensuring the domination of tribal populations whose allegiance to the former Ming dynasty had been one of the major obstacles in their conquest of China. The implementation of this policy meant, in fact, the end of the independence of the border peoples. To avoid when possible direct tribal opposition, this policy was preceded by attempts to undermining and eliminating native rulers, increase Chinese influence, improve infrastructure, and promote migration.

It is surprising that among the fierce Naxi warriors the loss of their independence was implemented with almost a complete lack of violence. This can be explained in this way: The border character of Lijiang and its strategic situation between China and Tibet made necessary to the Qing emperors to implement quickly and smoothly the new policy that would strength their control of the whole region. (In other regions of Yunnan the *tusi* system survived until the 20th century). In 1723, when disturbances in Tibet forced the Chinese to take a more active role in the affairs of their western borderlands, they found a good pretext in the bad government of Mu Kings that were in those years in a decadent mode, and having lost long ago their conquering impetus, reported no benefit to the imperial government. Official histories tell that some Naxi nobles asked the Chinese government to put an end to the rule of the Mu kings, of which they denounce their despotic character, that oppressed the people, accusing them of be violent, cruel, greedy and lustful. They must have lost the favour of their people, because, while in some indigenous territories the attempts to end the *tusis'* rule were followed by some of the bloodiest wars in 18th century China, among the Naxi, the deposition and dispossession of the Mu kings was carried out in a surprising peaceful way (Rock 1947: 46). Years before enmity had surged between the Lijiang kings and the powerful viceroy of Sichuan Province due to some administrative reforms intended to include Batang and other territories under the rule of the Mu kings. In 1720, king Mu Hing was asked to join an expedition to Tibet, and on route the Naxi army had some arguments with a protegé of the viceroy of Sichuan, which was killed. When later Mu Hing knew that he was a man of the viceroy and that the latter has already accused him before the emperor, he tried to return to

Lijiang, but got sick and died. His son and his nephew also died without descendants. The power was passed to Mu Zhong (Bacot 1913). Immediately, the Provincial Governor ordered him to collect back taxes from Jianchuan. When he fell short of the anticipated amount, the governor dismissed him after only 40 days of rule and confiscated his property to make up the balance. The Mu were formally, and finally, ousted (Goodman 1997: 31). The rule of the Naxi over their lives was put to an end. Lijiang County was established in 1770, and was ruled by Chinese's magistrates on behalf of the emperor until the end of dynastic rule in 1911.

Yang Bi, the first magistrate, built a wall around Lijiang, as a way to adapt the city to the Chinese standards, but the wall was destroyed by an earthquake in the following years. The new policy for ethnic minorities allowed the Han to interfere directly in matters of local custom where it was inconsistent with Confucian morality. "Four schools opened in Lijiang in 1736; their purpose was to effect a moral transformation of local subjects through education. The schools taught the Chinese language as well as Confucian ritual and ceremonial etiquette. Emphasis was placed on marriage and funerary ritual" (Chao 2008: 107). Sweeping changes were announced: cremation was to be replaced by burial and the old marriage based on free choice was abolished in favour of parent-arranged matches and Chinese-style weddings. The result was an alarming rate of female suicides, as the Confucian style marriage arranged by the parents was totally opposed to the native custom of free choice (Jackson 1979: 36, 17). With the effective incorporation of Lijiang into the Chinese empire, migration of peoples from other regions dramatically increased, mainly single men, as even by the end of the 19th century the imperial court did not allow Han women to emigrate to border regions. Mass immigration of single men into Naxi territory was a source of conflicts, as immigrants needed both land and women (Mathieu 2003: 341, 347). Qing's officials did not extend their authority very far into the peripheral hill regions, limiting the implementation of these reforms to parts of Lijiang City. We know from the first western travelers that visited the Naxi in the first years of the 20th century that Lijiang was famous for the hospitality of its women who offered themselves to the travelers, that the Chinese were still trying to put an end to the sexual freedom of the people, and that they still cremated their dead, finding in Lijiang a conspicuous lack of tombs (Bacot 1913: 11).

Trade developed quickly in Lijiang. Some Naxi merchants went deep into the snowy hinterlands to trade with the Tibetans. The most famous among them was Li Yue, who arrived in Lhasa in the second half of the 18th century. He brought large groups of Tibetan merchants to Yunnan and encouraged the Naxi merchants to trade with Tibet. They traversed the mountain ranges camping outdoors, paying little regards to the weather conditions to reach Lhasa three to four months later, climbed the Himalayan Range at 6.000 m, and at last they arrived at Kalimpang in northern India, only to organize themselves for the return trip carrying goods from Calcutta (Zhang and He 2005: 44- 45).

Lijiang was badly affected by the Panthay Rebellion, the Moslem uprising that during nearly 20 years (1856—1873) kept an independent power in Yunnan Province. In 1873, after the defeat of their main forces, the Qing troops set fire to

Lijiang in retaliation for the Mu family's alleged support of the Muslim Revolt (Goodman 1997: 50). It is possible that some families migrated, flying the Muslims, to Burma and later to Laos, where French researchers found what they thought could be Naxi populations.

The arrival of the modern world

In 1911 the last emperor of the Qing dynasty was deposed and the Republic of China was proclaimed. In 1912, in accordance with the assimilation goals of the new republic, the county government organized a Chinese Language Society to teach Naxi men Chinese language, and regulations were promulgated so that indigenous Naxi caught speaking their native language would be fined one copper coin (Track 1996: 141 in Rees 2000: 38). The assimilationists aims of the Republican government encouraged the political and social elite of Lijiang to be conversant with Chinese language and customs, with a particular impetus for the adoption of Chinese cultural institutions and the rejection of "feudal" elements and "superstitious" ceremonies (Rees 2000: 119).

In 1936 Japan invaded China. Japanese troops quickly conquered Nanjing, the capital, forcing the republican government to fly to Chongqing. With the main trade routes in the east of China completely blocked by the Japanese, the traditional trade routes with Tibet and India flourished: Lijiang became a prosperous city where banks and commercial enterprises were established, and goods were forwarded to Dali and the rest of China. When the United States entered war with Japan and the Sino-Japanese war became part of the

Second World War, the traditional trans-Himalayan trade routes were complemented by the military assistance of the American Volunteer Group, also known as the Flying Tigers. General Joseph "Vinegar Joe" Stillwell built Baisha Airport, about ten kilometers north of Lijiang, and from there American pilots flew hundreds of missions over the Himalayan passes, bringing supplies from India. So many planes were lost flying "the Hump" that the mountains were known as the "Tin Hills."

After the establishment of the People's Republic of China in 1949, immediate changes took place in Naxi society. The bucolic society described by Western travelers suddenly disappeared, giving room to a new vision of the world in which class contradictions were patent. The anger of the overtaxed peasantry was directed against the leisured classes, and most of the latter's property and privileges were taken away. Land reform was completed in 1953; it was followed by socialist transformation in agriculture, handicrafts and commerce. Finally, a whole new city grew up all around old Lijiang, containing mostly Han immigrants working in government agencies and economic development projects (Goodman 1997: 41). The name Naxi was officially approved in 1954[8]. The Lijiang Naxi Autonomous County was established in April

---

[8] Historically the Naxi have variously been called the Moxi, Luxi, Nari, Nahen, etc. "Naxi" also came to represent divergent groups: Han Chinese from Jiangnan who migrated during the Ming and Qing; other indigenous groups who migrated to Lijiang during the Qing and were forced to adopt the surname "He" as a marker of their subjugation to the Mu *tusi*; as well as peoples (called Lulu and Moso) who lived in contiguous areas (Chao 2008: 109).

1961 (Ma Yin 1989: 294). Without time to adapt to the new social conditions imposed by the new regime, the Cultural Revolution was launched in 1966, and was soon attacking any manifestation of the old, the traditional or the ethnic. Lijiang, being so accessible, was particularly vulnerable. Most of the temple's murals were totally destroyed, with only the damaged paintings at Baisha left as testimony to the savagery of the iconoclasts. In the countryside, the religious texts, objects and art works of the Dongba were confiscated and destroyed, sometimes even publicly burnt. Impossibility to practice their religion led some Naxi to suicide. Traditional orchestral music was forbidden as were the Naxi festivals. And countless Naxi suffered unjust imprisonment (Goodman 1997: 41).

After 1978 life slowly recovered its rhythm, but 30 years of reforms and revolutions have inevitably transformed old Naxi society. The lift of rules against religious activities and the development of tourism brought an authentic revival of traditions that one century ago were considered doomed to disappear. Massive migration of Han Chinese and the millions of visitors that every year travel to Lijiang, constitute new challenges to a tradition and culture that in the past was able to absorb and grow together with outside influences.

CHAPTER 3

Gods and Dongbas:
Naxi
Religion

The Naxi believe that the world is populated by multitude of spirits. These spirits, of different sizes, characters and disposition, can cause harm or provide benefits to human beings. Mountains and rivers, hills, lakes, trees and groves, all have their particular spirits. Spirits determine the shift of the seasons, night following day, the natural rhythm of life that leads to aging and death, and the alternation of winds and clouds. The territorial abode of these spirits is a mystery for the common human that can inadvertently disturb them or trespass upon their property and cause their anger, as these spirits are believed to have feelings, suffer from hunger or feel cold, and are therefore capable of bad or good behavior (Xi 2002: 79). The Naxi believe that the spirits of the human beings survive after death, lingering not far from their living descendants. Ancestors could be approached in time of a severe crisis in the family when, for example, someone is dangerously ill. The religious activities of the Naxi are focused on regulating the relationship of those unknown powers with the world of the living beings, to avoid the dangers that these spirits could cause to the living, and eventually to use their powers for their own benefit (Goullart 1957: 233).

Joseph Rock (1947: 204) thought that the Naxi were "exceedingly superstitious" and that religion was to them "a matter of outward behavior rather than an inward conviction", a materialistic view of the spiritual beings that defied Western conceptions. Goullart (1957: 147) considered that they "utilize the religious options available to them according to their needs, with each religion serving some particular need:" Ancestor worship to keep up the contact with the departed, animism to deal with the unseen powers of Nature, shamanism for the protection of the living and dead from the evil spirits. "On top of these religious beliefs, they had a deep-rooted and eminently practical Epicurean philosophy. It taught them that this was, indeed, a transient plane of existence but nevertheless very material and substantial" (Goullart 1957: 147).

This factual relationship of the Naxi with the spirits can be framed as an instance of the ritualistic religion common to the Chinese world, where "ritual performance and belief are not distinguished. It means that the separation of belief from performance is inappropriate, because the participants act in the belief that their actions will have bureaucratic efficacy" (Feuchtwang 2001: 7, 10, 11). That is, they believe that there are some spirits that can harm human beings; and when the specialists who can communicate with them (*llubhu*) recommend performing a ceremony, they request a Dongba priest, who is invested with some powers, to do it. The Naxi believe that most undesirable states such as misfortune, illness, quarreling, suicide, death, and other breaches of social harmony are caused by demons or bad spirits, and that to revert these undesirable states the bad spirits must be driven away or killed. First they must know the nature of the demon that causes problems. This is the task of the *llubhu*, who reaching trance is thought to be able to communicate with the spirits. Once known the nature of the demon causing problems, he must be driven away: the task of the Dongba, who to do this must have power (Jackson 1979: 207).

The Dongba[9] priests are the protagonists of the Dongba religion, a ritual mediation between humans and spirits developed over the course of the centuries. They propitiate or exorcise spirits and demons performing rituals, in which they chant a ritual text with the help of manuscripts written in the pictographic Dongba script. The name Dongba refers to various related but different concepts: Naxi traditional religion, the script in which the texts of this religion are written, the collection of these texts (the Dongba Classics) and the ritual specialist who read these texts (Jackson 1979: 18).

Dongba religion is characterized by the lack of a structure, temples, canon, and full-time specialists. Dongbas, however, are credited with some of the most brilliant successes in human history: the creation and use of a pictographic language, the writing of thousands of sacred scriptures in this language, the creation of scroll paintings of more than 10 meters long, and the development of an ancient dance notation. In the Dongba scriptures there is information about the old Naxi society and the way it evolved, and also about astronomy, meteorology, calendar, technology, zoology,

---

[9] Dtomba, and other variants of the name of the main ritual specialists among the Naxi, are transcribed as Dongba.

botany, metallurgy, husbandry, and the original philosophy, history, folklore and religion of the Naxi (He Zhiwu 1987: 33).

According to Naxi religion, there are three places for the dead: heaven for those who die a normal death, hell for those who are wicked, and the Third Kingdom of Jade Dragon Mountain for some special deaths. The procedure to send the dead to heaven, called *sashakou*, is to insert a red pack, made of silk or paper with certain grains of rice (nine for male or seven for female), some tea leaves, and few small pieces of gold and silver into the dying person's mouth before his or her last breath (Sangde). Those who suffer an unnatural death are transformed after their decease into evil or ferocious demons, because having no chance to receive *sashakou*, their souls cannot enter the gate of heaven to meet their ancestors. Instead, they may be tortured with the scorching of hellfire or drift with the wind forever as homeless souls. These wandering souls can make trouble, cause people to fall sick and suffer disasters, menace the development of livestock, harm the growth of crops, confuse the minds of people and especially entice young people to tread the pernicious path to destruction by love suicide or violent death (He and He 1998). To prevent people from being haunted by these souls, it is necessary that the family of the dead invites Dongba masters to hold a *Harlalluku* rite in order to send the drifting soul to the Jade Dragon Mountain, a "third state," as a paradise between heaven and hell (Sangde).

Shu spirits of nature

Among the many spirits of nature the Shu[10] serpent spirits are the most prominent and important. They are water spirits that inhabit also high mountains, spurs, alpine meadows, trees, rocks, cliffs, fields, villages, houses, and the ground on which the houses are built. As the snakes make their appearance with the rainy season the Shu are considered responsible for rain, with the power also to impart fecundity and grant numerous offspring. Being also the guardians of riches, they are constantly implored to grant wealth, full-grain boxes, livestock, and of all else, long life (Rock 1952). They are easily offended if a man trespass on their rights, when they may steal one of the man souls, causing him to fall ill and even to die. The beliefs about the Shu are complex and far-reaching; their popularity derives partly from their power to grant fertility and riches and partly because they can steal men's souls and cause them to sicken and die (Jackson 1979: 102). As in the Shu the beneficial and disastrous effects of nature are embodied, the Naxi developed rituals to thank them for their help and to avoid their bad influence (Mu 2005: 63).

According to Naxi myths, men and Shu are brothers from the same mother and different fathers. They separated the realms of their dominions, but as later men continuously trespassed into the Shu territory (mountains and rivers), enmity surged and many fights happened. Dongba Shiluo was then called to descent from heaven to act as a mediator and restore peace and harmony between man and Shu. With his help they reached an agreement. Human beings must be moderate in using the nature and hold "worshipping the Shu god of nature"

---

[10] Also known in the ethnological literature regarding the Naxi as Ssu, Su, Nagas, dragons, etc.

ceremonies every year, and the Shu would opportunely provide natural things to human beings and stop attacking them. In this way, their brotherly relation was restored, and they lived friendly generation after generation (He and He 1999: 36).

Contact with the Shu is subject to the same level of equality as contact between people, being the Shu a reflection of the human beings. If a family is a rich or poor, if any of the members is lame, or blind, the Shu they worship would be rich or poor, lame, or blind (Mu 2005). Humans take richness from Shu as part of their daily activities, cutting down trees, hunting and storing and using water, and then pay back to them by means of religious rituals aimed to maintain the balance between human beings and the natural environment. There are many taboos that protect the places where Shu are worshipped, which remind the people the dangers of not respecting nature (Mu 2005). The most important of the Shu rituals, performed at the village level on a dragon or snake day in the second month of the lunar calendar, is called "repayment of debt to Shu." A constant reminder to the Naxi that humankind must control its appetites, not taking from nature more than it should, and that the more a community takes from its environment the more it must return to the Shu (Xi 2002: 79-80). The ceremony, usually performed nearby the water source of the village, is an enactment of the agreement reached in mythical times between men and nature with the help of Dongba Shiluo, and a call to the need to preserve this harmony. During the three days that it lasts the people pray the Shu spirits to forgive all their past transgressions and to provide good luck (Li Jingshen 1991).

The myths and ceremonies related with the worship of the Shu show that the Naxi knew since long the need to keep the equilibrium between man and nature, in order to ensure the sustainability of the agricultural production. Their emphasis in their brotherhood means that if men harm their Shu nature brother, they are harming themselves. A call for a moderate use of the natural resources, for not polluting the sources of water, not felling trees indiscriminately, and not hunting in excess. The ceremony serves to reinforce the need to keep the ecological balance as a personal and collective compromise. A compromise really successful, as seen in the fact that before the "economic development" promoted after 1949, most of the Naxi territory was covered with forests (Li Jingshen 1991). Worship to Shu reveals the thought that to get the fruits of nature (animal or vegetal) is to cause a wound to the earth, and that human beings must repay for this wound (Mu 2005: 61).

The Shu nature spirits have the head of a frog, the body of a human, and the coils of a snake, frogs and snakes being regarded as their children (Xi 2002: 81-82). The Shu, which control the rain and are full of life-giving power, are closely associated with feminine, and worshipped as feminine deities, manifestations of the spirit of the Great Earth symbolizing motherhood (Xi 2002: 84). As the earth is the mother from which all life is born, nature is regarded as a mother and placed high in human esteem, holy and sacrosanct, a position that implies a kind of unity with untouched nature, symbiotic and of mutual benefit (Xi 2002: 93). The principal goal of Shu worship is to ask for rainwater and offspring. Offspring must come from the primary matrix or mother body,

76

water is the source from which all life is nurtured, the place where the Shu deities reside, from where they dominate the heaven and earth, with everything belonging to human beings having been granted by them.

Jackson considers that "the actions which arouse the Shu's displeasure sound like a strictly interpreted law of property rights. The prohibited actions are all those which infringe upon the prerogatives of the chiefs" (1979: 251-3). Mathieu frames the Shu nature spirits' worship in the struggle to control the spiritual realms of the new domains continuously conquered by the Mu kings. Yang Fuquan view that they reflect the wisdom of the Naxi people that, at an early age discovered the need to preserve the harmony between man and nature, connects maybe better with the dozens of narrations where the pollution of the sacred nature by the human beings has no direct relationship with the economical use of nature; a concept on the other side common to ethnic groups cultural and linguistically related to the Naxi.

The brotherhood between humans and Shu could be a development of the Naxi brotherhood with their original totems: frog, snake, monkey and bear. Frog and snake would become the Shu, while bear and monkey would become ancestors. The Naxi call their ancestors "monkeys". The relationship between human beings and snakes is very close. When a snake is found at home, it is believed to be an ancestor returning. They hold the snake with a stick and put milk or butter on its body, then they take it out and set it free in the wild. A snake found in other circumstances is usually killed, but this killing is considered also a way to allow the spirit of the ancestor to travel to his proper place. Because they believe that after dead the human will become snakes, which in turn when cremated will become ancestors; the cremation pit being called "the place where the snake skin is changed" (Mu 2005:21-22). Nature deities are born from the Shu that govern different natural accidents and phenomena; ancestral deities are ancestors veneered as great hunters or warriors, which with the development of the patriarchal power, became the creators of the world and of all what exists (Mu 2005: 236).

That human beings are inseparable part of nature is shown in the Naxi belief that every person has a Sv life god, that is, a personal share of the Shu that animate everything in nature. The Shu serpent spirits could steal a man's soul in order to punish him for any offense, that is, to recall back to Nature the share given to this person at birth. Without his Sv Life god a man falls ill (Jackson 1979: 245). That means that the share of the nature soul provided a person at birth is returned to nature at the end of his life. This spiritual unity of man and nature can help to understand their respect for the environment, their ideas about the brotherhood between men and nature, and the cosmological unity that is shown in their main myths. "From the fact that people worship their own Sv rather than their own soul, it is evident that there is a concept of the divine within one's own body" (Oppitz and Hsu 1998: 207). Sv is the collective spirit of each person and his totemic ancestors, all born from the same mother, Sv spirits can divide and marry and turn into the Sv of other family or lineage (Mu 2005:77). After death, Sv is transformed in the snake totem to be ready to become ancestor again. Naxi people consider that a man is adult at 13 because they have already lived and passed through a cycle of the 12 elements, and is considered to have a

Sv life god that must be present also in the family Sv god basket. After the coming on age ritual his soul become part of the family soul, that links all them with the totemic ancestors and inhabits the Sv god basket, and after death his soul can be send to the ancestors' lands. Death of a person is the death of his Sv life god and the beginning of a series of changes that will turn him into an ancestor, which will travel to their sacred lands and, eventually, maybe due to Buddhist influences, reborn in the world. The life of a person is, for the Naxi, the nurturing of his share of the family Sv life god inside them (Mu 2005 38-39).

This contradictory relationship between men and nature is impregnated with Taoist ideas. "Man is primarily a part of nature, but he is a part of nature which is made opposed to nature through a process of alienation. He is always intentionally acting against nature." On the other side, man knows that "he should not try to interfere with the course of nature but should always be conscious that he himself is an integral part of nature, even in obedience to its rules." Knowing that the more than one tries to control the course of nature, the further one runs contrary to it, Naxi solved in a practical way a contradiction that lurked above Chinese culture from the first philosophical thoughts (He and Peng 2009: 237, 240). Opposition between Shu and human beings is a reflection of the opposition between heaven-made and man-made, nature and society, developed by the ancient Taoist philosopher Zhuangzi. Taoist also believe that the spiritual souls tend to wander, "and any passion or desire can result in loss of soul" (Kuiper 2011: 101). The Dongba must be considered the spiritual healer with the power to restore the equilibrium inside the sick person.

Spirits of places and Sanduo god

Sanduo is the god of war, the main protector of the Naxi people. He was invoked in the past before entering combat. In a manuscript preserved in the Beiyue Temple he is called the creator of the universe, the defender of peace, the protector against calamities such as fires, floods, plagues and wars. He is eulogized by saying that his power is as high as Heaven, his light shines like lightning, his mouth spits fire, and his body is as white as snow. Legends tell of his mysterious appearances, wearing a white dress and riding a white horse, that led the Mu family troops to their victories. The worship of Sanduo, the most important of territorial deities, is somehow related to the worship of the Shu. Both share their magical functions, and both contribute to give the Naxi rulers the right to rule over lands that were previously inhabited by another peoples, and where the spirits of the ancestors of these peoples, were, even after the arrival of the Naxi, their powerful masters. Both Sanduo and Shu are worshipped on the second month, just before the start of the agricultural activities that would provide the Naxi with the fruits of the conquered land. The ceremonies held at two different centers of the Naxi realm are quite diverse; while in the spiritual center of Baidi the Shu are worshipped on a snake or dragon day, near the political center of Baisha, Sanduo is worshipped in a sheep day. Baidi is the sacred place of the Dongba priest, where Dongba Shiluo is worshipped; Baisha, that of the *llubhu* shamans (originally shamanesses), that consider Sanduo their patron.

It was the custom for the ruling chief of the Naxi to come to the Beiyue Temple on the 8th day of the second moon to worship Sanduo (Rock 1947: 193). The people that live far from Lijiang usually worship him in a local temple in their own villages (Yang 1999). Sanduo is the name the Tibetans gave to Lijiang. That suggests the existence of a spiritual relation between the city, the Jade Dragon Mountain and the Sanduo God that protects the city. Beiyue is the name given in Nanzhao to the Jade Dragon Mt, when it was associated with the North Mountain. Legends tell that the temple is erected in the place where a magic white stone stopped to move. White stones also protect the Qiang. The huge Jade Dragon Mountain with its white snow can be perceived as a huge white stone (He Zhiwu 1987: 46).

Religious specialists

Among the Naxi there are different kinds of ritual specialists with the task of identifying and correcting the imbalances in the state of the cosmos that can affect human existence causing sickness and various disasters. To identify the cause of imbalance they usually resort to divination, which originally was the exclusive task of woman diviners or *paq*, and now is one of the main activities of the Dongbas. Once the cause of the problem has been determined, it can be corrected in a shamanistic way, when the *llubhu* "confronts the afflicting demon directly by journeying to that part of the cosmos where the demon dwells" (McKhann cited in Rees 2000: 35), in a

81

ritual way, when one or more Dongba priests are called in order to perform the necessary corrective ritual, or by a combination of both: As many Dongba also act as *llubhu* and they not only perform the ritual prescribed in their scriptures but reach trance and confront directly the demons and spirits. Before the term Dongba was put into use, there were some ritual offices as *biuq* or *biubbiuq*, the main ritualist considered the old Dongbas, whose task is related to the Tibetan Bonpos, Yi *bimos* and other ritual specialists who exorcize through chanting, *ddaheeq*, or priest who performs at the ceremonies to open the way and other funerary rites, and *xusui*, who performed at the Sacrifice to Heaven (Mathieu 2003: 117, He Zhiwu 1993: 2). The *paq* diviners were the oldest religious specialist, later called *sunyi* or *llubhu*, also women at first, which can divine thanks to the grace of Pangzusamei, the goddess of divination. Chinese influence started to give more importance to men in religious affairs, that became *llhubu* shamans, and *bimo* or *piuq* ritualist, who later were conferred by the people the honorific title of Dongba or master.

Dongba priests

The word Dongba or dto-mba is of Tibetan origin, meaning "teacher, founder or promulgator of a particular doctrine." They are the priests of Naxi primitive religion. Other etymology assures that the dto in their name indicates followers of Dongba Shiluo, and mba means to chant in a loud voice. The Dongba have a deep knowledge of the traditional culture of the Naxi; they master ancient Naxi pictographs, know Dongba scriptures, have the gift of singing and dancing, are

Naxi religious specialists in Dongba script, from left to right:
Dongba, lama, paq or diviner, and llubhu or shamaness.

good at painting, weaving, making mud figures or wood-
carving; they can write poems, perform divination, and have
the ability of performing varied religious rituals. Ordinarily,
the knowledge of the Dongba is handed down from within the
family, from father to son if possible, or from uncle to nephew,
but sometimes the aspirant to be Dongba can seek instruction
from a master. The Dongba must be invited to hold rituals or
do divination while building a house, giving birth, naming
children, curing illness or death, marriage, funeral, on New
Year's Day or other festivals, and even for going on a journey or
hunting. Dongba priests are generally farmers that live among
the common people and are familiar not just with the rituals,
divinations and pictographic manuscripts of their religion, but
with the customs of daily life, herbal medicine, handicrafts, and
traditional architecture. Only when performing their rituals
they act as intermediaries between gods, men and ghosts.
Though they enjoy a high social position, there is no difference
of status among them, but the level of knowledge, skill,
generations and fame. Dongbas with outstanding memory are

able to chant several hundreds of manuscripts which they have learnt by heart (Yang 2003: 480; Li and A 1998; He and He 1999).

All Naxi villages had more than one Dongba because some ceremonies involve several of them performing. They have no specific religious organization, uniform rules or regulations, no temples or monasteries. The Dongba are cultural specialists who transmit and develop the traditional knowledge and spiritual values of the Naxi. They are also key persons in the conservation of nature that promote a harmonious relationship between man and nature, based in the sustainable use of natural resources. Dongba culture includes an encyclopedia of social life, religious philosophy, history, folklore, science and technology, medicine, literature and art. With about 100 offering sacrifices and rituals with more than 1,000 kinds of scriptures put in use, Dongba religion functions as the vehicle of traditional education of the people, as religious ceremonies are part of marriages, funerals, births and deaths (Yang 2003: 479; Yang 1999: 84)

The social and political stature of the Dongbas was very high in ancient times, when as intermediaries between humans and the spiritual world they were considered wise men with knowledge about heaven and earth, acting as counselors and advisors of the tribe and clan chieftains (Yang 2003: 480). It is possible that they even enjoyed the political and ritual leadership of their clans, performing divination before the main activities of the community. Later they were stripped of all their power, becoming peasants among peasants and herders among herders (Mu 1991). The fall of the Dongba priests could have been part of the political movements of the Mu kings to consolidate their dominion over the Naxi people. According to their level of training, we find two kinds of Dongbas, the small Dongbas or part-time specialists, living humble lives in their own villages, catering for the spiritual needs of their folks; and the great Dongbas, who have knowledge of more ceremonies, made use of a wider range of ritual objects, acted as masters of other Dongbas, and in the past performed the kingly ritual and ceremonies. All Great Dongbas are considered fully initiated after they have studied with the Dongba Masters in the sacred site of Baidi (Mathieu 2003: 116).

Performing their ceremonies the Dongbas usually wear a

Five lobes hat of the Dongba

ritual dress, with a peculiar five-lobed crown (the *ko*) that invests them with the domain over the five directions. The *ko* crown is made of leather or papier-maché, and is tied with a band in the back of the head. At the top of each segment is the figure of Saluwede, the supreme god of the Naxi, and the Garuda bird with outspread wings. In the center there are images of five deities, the central one being Dongba Shilou. Sometimes they wear a curious forked iron helmet like those of

85

the Bon priests and shell necklaces. When dancing, they carry a small gong in one hand and a wooden sword in the other, and they blow conch-shell trumpets (Jackson 1979: 93).

The main rituals of the Dongba religion resemble shamanistic traditions present in the area. The first Dongbas were called "those who dance and sing," which remind us the Yi *bimo*, "the master of dance" (Jackson 1979: 63). The title of *bimo*, similar to that of the ritual specialists of the Yi, Lisu and Hani, may reflect a time before the arriving of the Dongba tradition, when the culture of the Naxi forefathers was not so clearly differentiated from that of other peoples linguistically related to them (Guo 1991). Besides the *bimo* these ethnic groups have also a shaman with abilities to travel to the realm of the spirits called *sanyi*. It is possible that with the arrival of Bon priests, expelled from Tibet, to the Naxi territory the Dongba priest could have usurped the role of the *bimo*, because their beliefs, cultural objects, spiritual perceptions, and ritual forms, seem related to those of the Bon.

The Dongbas shamanistic rituals to expel the evil spirits who cause illness of the body involve sacrifices, trance dancing to the accompaniment of drums and gongs, and manipulation of fire and heated objects. Rock (1924: 487) described that at the climax of some ceremonies he "dips his right hand into the hot oil, holding the pot in his bare left hand, enters the room where the banners are, and emerges with the pot full of blue flames, which he stirs with his sword; then dips his hand into the fiery pot. With his burning pot and flame-dripping fingers he rushes from room to room, sword in mouth, driving out the devil, who may be cowering somewhere in a nook. The throng of onlookers now becomes excited and directs attention to this corner and that as not yet purified. Obediently the Dongba rushes with his flaming pot and fire-spouting fingers to the places directed, until finally he sprinkles with fire the circular altar, which is quickly taken up and rushed out of the courtyard and burned amid the popping of firecrackers. The flaming Dongba follows the altar to the accompaniment of the beating of gongs and drums and iron rings. The women now hastily pick up brooms and sweep out every corner of the courtyard, to be certain that nothing remains, after which the doors are closed, and the sick man is supposed to be relieved of the evil one and consequently of his ailment."

The first descriptions of Naxi ceremonies suggest that the trance was reached through hours of frenetic dance under the sound of a drum. The widespread cultivation of opium in those years and the deep knowledge of nature plants by the Dongba make it possible that their experience was facilitated by some substances. The only reference to a possible use of natural substances to enhance their shamanistic powers is provided by Bacot: "The Dongbas drink a kind of tea before start their ceremonies. This tea allows them manipulate a red hot plowshare, to dance on the flames, to take a pot of boiling oil, or to throw fire with their hands" (1913: 22).

Dongba Shiluo, the patron god of the Dongba shamans, is the divine mediator that lies between men and their use of nature, to keep balance, or restore it when needed. The main ceremonies the Dongba shamans perform, acting always in the name of Dongba Shiluo, are the restoration or accumulation of the spirit of nature inside the human beings, be because they suffer an illness as a result of their lost of their share of the Shu soul of nature, be as a mean to increase the strength of it and get long life, be in the funerary ceremonies when this Sv life god is compelled to give up the dead body and return to the ancestors' land. Shiluo is the dealer, the doctor, who must solve the unbalances inside human beings, at the same time part of the sacred spirit of nature, and in a contradictory relation with nature, as they need to destroy at least part of the nature to carry on their own material development. The thought that every person has the sacred inside him or her is reinforced by the myth that tracks the origin of the human beings back to the marriage of Congrenlien, the only survivor to the flood, with Cunhongbaobai, the daughter of the celestial god Zilao Apu. All humans share this heavenly mother, all have inside blood of gods, as all can trace their genealogies to the God of Heaven.

It is possible that a kind of pictographic script with ritual use preceded its use by the Dongba priests, as it seems to be part of the cultural background common to the Qiang peoples. The recourse to the painting of signs to be used as a mnemonic device to drive the ritualist along a religious ceremony is common also among the Yi, Lisu, Jingpo and other ethnic groups related to the Naxi, being the Naxi the more developed and standardized of these systems of signs. The sacredness of images is widespread in the entire Chinese world; images being sometimes considered the embodiment of the deity depicted.

Dongba religion was developed in Baidi by Dongba Shiluo and Aming Shiluo, who started to write books with pictographic characters. At first most of the Dongba were from the Baidi area only, later, Dongba surged in many places, but only those who had study in Baidi were great Dongbas. Most of the Dongba distinctions are related to staying or not in Baidi, to have performed the acquisition of power ceremony or not, to belong to an old lineage of Dongba or not. In the Dongba ceremonies there is a clear division between the Dongbas who can take charge of a ritual and those who cannot, called *pyza* or helpers (Li Guowen 1993).

About 1554 the Naxi king Mu Gao went to Baidi, where he wrote a short poem about a wise man that lived in a cave 500 years before. He Zhiwu identifies this saint with Aming Shiluo, which must have lived there about the 1050s. According to the legends Aming Shiluo belonged to the Ye lineage. He went to Tibet, learned the Tibetan language and writing, and when he came back to Baidi, retired to study in a cave. He is credited with having created the Dongba religion and the pictographs. Later he became the second master in the tradition after the founder Dongba Shiluo, and every Dongba must go to Baidi to get the magic power from him (He Zhiwu 1987: 31). The Dongba cults in this time must have not been very popular in Lijiang; otherwise the king would have differentiated them from the Buddhist faith. Maybe they were unknown outside Baidi, and the sudden propagation of their faith coincided in time with the Bon expulsion from Tibet, and their expansion from their base in Naxi lands as a kind of local-flavoured Bon: the Dongba religion.

Other legends date the life of Aming Shiluo in the 13th and the 17th centuries, and narrate his acquisition of magic powers after a secret apprenticeship as a servant in the house of a lama, and the steal of the sacred books after training the lama horses to not be able to cross beyond the bridge that led to his lands. Hidden in a cave in his home town, for fear of the revenge of the powerful lama, he developed the rituals of the Dongba religion. In his legends is suggested that the title of Dongba antedates him. In the Mu kings' court he performed acts of magic that surpassed those of other magicians, with

supernatural feats as understanding the language of the birds, that pointed to him as a true shaman (He and Yang 1993:

216). He was the first person to bring Dongba religion to Lijiang. He opened schools in Baisha, where he standardized Naxi pictographs, and wrote the first Dongba scriptures, acquiring many disciples over time (Lee 2003: 12). Dongba religion, at least in its first steps, was not well considered by the Mu kings, as the several recorded attempts to kill Aming Shiluo show. The humble origin of Dongba religion is perceived in the sacred feats of Aming Shiluo, his work as a servant, his theft of the sacred books, and the need to hide in a cave to save his own life.

Llubhu shamans

The *llubhu* (also called *sunyi*) are the Naxi sorcerers or sorceresses. In ancient days they were always women, mediums who went into trances and claimed to see ghosts, the spirit of the deceased persons. They have the power of dealing with ghost and demons, to cast horoscopes and to enter in communication with the dead. The pictograph for a *llubhu* depicts a seated woman with flowing hair; they were consulted to divine the causes of misfortune, to speak to the dead, and to drive out demons while in trance (Jackson 1979: 57). The name *llubhu* could also be translated as "wife of llu"; being the llu-mun the serpent spirits also known as Shu[11]. This could

---

[11] Llu also means arrow and an arrow is used to symbolize Sv, the Life god; these two Shu and Sv are intimately related. The ubiquity and uniqueness of the Shu mythology in Naxi belief make it extremely probable that this was an ancient set of ideas connected with shamanism (Jackson 1979: 259)

explain the feminine character of the *llubhu* as well as their ability to enter in communication with the spirits of nature.

Goullart (1957: 234) tells that the visit of the *llubhu* was always arranged in the middle of the night, when the neighbours were asleep. He chanted the incantations from the scriptures, accompanying himself on a small drum. He danced a little. Then he fell into a trance. There was no direct voice. The man gasped out what he saw. It might, for instance, be a tall old man in a purple jacket, slightly lame, leaning on a black stick. "Oh, that is Grandfather!" cried the family, prostrating themselves. Then the sickness of the patient was described. "The old man is smiling," reported the *sunyi*. "He says the boy will recover in seven days if he takes this medicine". *Sunyi* is a disrespectful term for a *llubhu*, in which the symbols for blood and penis were used, which either hints at sexual orgies in connection with the worship of Sanduo, their patron deity, or could be insulting defamation. In fact, the term "nyi" means to heal or cure so it could refer to the healers of the mountain god; this is more plausible because of the close resemblance between the term *sanyi* and the name of the Yi shaman (Jackson 1979: 397).

In the old Naxi society there was probably a sexual division of religious tasks, with female shamans responsible for divination and male priests for ritual. Old Dongba manuscripts suggest that in the past women were considered smarter and enjoyed a superior position than men. They knew the essential divination techniques, they could choose the types of rituals in accordance with the results of the divination, and they were more often possessed by spirits than the men. With the establishment of the male-dominated society divination and rituals were performed mainly by men. Women were banned from the public arena and religious rituals, and treated as if they were possessed by evil spirits instead (Xi 1999). In the real practice the activities of the Dongba and the *llubhu* are not clearly differentiated. Many Dongbas acted also as *llubhu*, performing a symbolic change of costume when they exchanged roles (He and Yang 1993: 191).

The *llubhu* also have their special ritual paraphernalia. They wear a long blue dress with a belt and a red turban; their sacred instruments include a sword, a small gong, some iron bells and rings, and a small drum hanging from their neck (Guo 1998: 326). They are not attached to Dongba Shiluo but to Sanduo, the divine spirit of the Jade Dragon Mountain. The candidate to be *llubhu* must have the capacity for sustained dissociation or self-hypnosis if he is to carry out the exploits demanded of him: licking red-hot plough shares, dipping his hands in boiling oil and setting them alight, etc. Many *llubhu* get the power to contact with the spirits after suffering a severe sickness. Then they will perform a ceremony to get their red band. They dance as crazy towards the Sanduo temple, where they must continue dancing frenetically before an image of Sanduo covered by a long red cloth. The prospective *llubhu* keeps dancing before the image, and if the red cloth falls over him, it means that Sanduo god accepts him as a *llubhu*, if not, he will be considered a person with mental problems, being the red band their distinctive mark.

The *llubhu* of Tacheng district are known as *sangpa*, they have some power stones of brilliant quartz. They can perform divination and face directly the spirits that cause a sickness. To heal a sick person they go into trance and directly confront the demons, they "leap into the bonfire and with his bare feet scatter the burning logs into the four corners of the courtyard" or show their magical skills spreading boiling oil with their hand around the courtyard, or even killing a small pig biting its back (Rock 1924: 19).

In the old Dongba manuscripts there is no title for the Dongba, existing only the *bimo* or ritualist, the *paq* or diviner, and the *llubhu* or shaman. Dongba in Tibetan means teacher, in Naxi dancer; it suggests that at some point in history the Naxi dancers, i.e. the *llubhu* shamans and the *bimo* ritualists, whose functions were similar to those of the Yi and other ethnic groups, embraced the Dongba Shiluo mediation in their rituals, the central point of the Dongba doctrine, and all of them became Dongbas. All them were called "master" and considered wise. As the Dongba were mainly responsible for ritual activities, they didn't need to have special psychological or spiritual powers. When *bimo* and *llubhu* made the powerful Dongba Shiluo their own ancestor, they tried to guarantee the efficacy of their ritual independently of the individual power of each one.

If these *bimo* ritualist farmers that were called after their day work to relieve the pain of their fellow citizens saw in the Dongba movement a chance to increase their efficacy, the *llubhu* shamans, always on the verge of a failure that could make them be considered crazy at the eyes of the people, saw in the Dongba mediation a chance to a socially respected position. They were the best fit among the Naxi to understand the ideas that underlie Dongba rituals. There are Dongbas who are at the same time *llubhus* because many *llubhus* choose to become Dongbas, Dongba being an honorific name and not a name that denotes a specific religious activity. Other religious specialists, *paq* or diviners, could have followed the same path. The Dongbas gradually displaced or converted other ritualists to their ritual techniques; in the end their efficacy was considered so high that they performed most of Naxi rituals. The fact that women cannot be Dongba explains that most of the *paq* were necessarily women, being the male *paq* possibly transformed into Dongbas. While the ritualist saw his power increased by the mediation of Dongba Shiluo, shaman and diviners saw their activities socially recognized. The local adaptation of deities belonging to cultures considered more advanced is a common act in China and the rest of the world. While Chinese influence was focused in the Mu court and the Naxi aristocracy, with their Buddhist and Confucian temples and their Taoist rituals, the Bon wizards had the same effect in the isolated Naxi villages. The people expected efficacy from the Dongba ritual, which helps understand that with the arrival of modern medicine they became diviners, or psychopomps, as today. This search for efficacy is shown in the first moments of the ceremony when the *llubhu* ask for the help of his protector deities, of his ancestors and even of the ancestors of the sick person, to get the power to heal (He and Yang 1993: 241).

Dongba religion and Bon

Dongba religion has many resemblances with the Tibetan Bon, with the names and legends of the master founder almost identical, as are the name of deities, rituals, and ritual instruments. The main gods of the Dongba are of Tibetan origin: as Iku Age and Saluwede, protector deities as the Garuda, the lion and the dragon, or the Shu nature spirits. There are Bon and Lamaist terms that can be found in the Dongba script. Their cosmogony and creation of the world are more or less the same. The rest of the creation myth, however, is related to other peoples of their same language stock (He Zhiwu 1989: 43).

The Dongba revere Dongba Shiluo as master and founder of their religion; his mythic exploits killing demons seem very much those of the historic creator of Bon, Shenrab mi-bo. The central point of Naxi philosophy, as transmitted in their manuscripts, is the belief in the Shu aquatic spirits that govern nature having the power of steal human souls. These Shu are the exact replica of the Tibetan "klu", divinities of the aquatic subsoil, which inhabiting each accident of the land did not admit being stolen by men. If anybody dislodges them, they will revenge punishing the culprit with terrible pains (Allanic 1994: 94). "Like Shenrab Mibo, Dongba Shiluo resided in heaven from where he descended to earth to suppress the multitude of demons that caused havoc among humanity" (Rubin 2011: 45). We cannot forget that the reformed Bon religion, that which arrived at Naxi lands, was a blending of the primitive Bon shamanism of the Tibetans, with latterly-added Buddhist elements. The primitive Bon could have had common points with beliefs held by other Tibeto-Burman speaking peoples. The belief in a kind of powerful nature spirits, called Shu among the Naxi, could be part of the culture common to geographically and linguistically related peoples: one ancestral spiritual heritage extending to most of East Asia, and as far as Siberia: "All forests, trees, waters and animals have spirits or 'Masters' by whom they are animated. In other words these trees, animals, etc. are vessels in which the spirits dwell" (Stutley 2002: 53).

The resemblances in the name of the Dongba and Bon ancestral master, their main deities, priests, and religious titles cannot hide that their character, birth and magical feats are different. Bon and Dongba could be considered original religions in which the main deities, rituals and religious specialists have similar but different meanings (Liu 1991).

The expulsion of the Bon monks from Tibet led to their dispersion among the Naxi, deeply influencing their rituals. Jackson thinks that if one progressively strips the Bon of its temples and books, ban its monks from their traditional begging as a means of revenue, proscribes them from gathering together in the main towns and villages, and leaves them for a few years, it will result in a peasant farmer with a fund of esoteric means of coping with demons – a Dongba. In order to write the Dongba books that person must know both written Tibetan and spoken Naxi apart from having a script to write it in. One type of person would be so qualified: a Naxi trained at Bon religion. The reason for writing down the rituals was primarily to remember the correct names and order of events, a Bon tradition that was important since a mistake would nullify the ritual. The idea that the first Dongbas were originally proscribed Bon monks explains the content and style of Naxi ritual. They wore the regalia of Bon monks and used their instruments in conducting the blood sacrifice while invoking a deified founder as mediator (Jackson 1979: 68- 72).

A comparison of Naxi religious texts with those of the Yi and other Tibeto-Burman speakers in Southwest China could provide information about Naxi old religion, the set of original beliefs that was later modified by their own history as well as by Chinese, Tibetan, and Mongolian influences. Among the oldest stratum of beliefs we find the existence of spirits that populate every section of the natural world, the ability of these spirits to harm people and cause sickness, the origin of these spirits in the souls of some death persons, the presence of rituals aimed at fighting these demons and recover the soul of the sick person, the existence of two main kinds of religious specialists: Priests performing the main rituals (sometimes with the help of a writing or symbols system) and shamans that can travel to the netherworld, identify the spirit that is causing a sickness and directly negotiate a positive solution. It is possible that some of these basic characteristics of the Tibeto-Burman ancient religion were common also to the old Bon of the Tibetans. Among the outside elements brought with the Bon the most important is the central role of Dongba Shiluo as mediator between the world of the humans and that of the spirits, and the Hindu mythological background, specially the victory of the Garuda over the Nagas, that seems to back the effectiveness of the Dongba actions. Most of the beliefs of Dongba religion were already part of Naxi religion. The Naxi Bon priests that revolutionized their religion with a sacred script and a completely new mythology only superimposed the Bon rituals over the preexistent structure. Doubtless the use of the new and complex ritual paraphernalia by the first Bon monks that became Dongbas was considered more developed and effective, pushing the rest of the Naxi priests to embrace their rituals. Identification of the Naxi Shu with the Bon klu, the Hindu Naga, or the Chinese Long are only approximate, they could also be identified with indigenous nature spirits of nearby ethnic groups, keeping however each of them different characteristics that can reflect their history and religious evolution. This victory of the Bon priests and the new ritual over the indigenous traditions can be reflected in the myth *The Battle of White and Black*, in which the victory of the white is seen as a contradiction, as in the Naxi language "black" is synonym of big, noble, vast. Among the Yi, Nu and old Qiang peoples the black was also the most loved colour. It is possible that black was the favorite colour of the ancient Naxi, but that due to the influence of the Tibetan Bon religion, white began to get preeminence and later became the most auspicious colour (Bai 1991).

Dongba deities

The Naxi people believe that every object, animal, plant, or natural phenomena has its own spirit. In the Dongba scriptures more than 2,400 spirits can be found. The sky, earth, sun, moon, mountains, water, wind, and even stones are all believed to be animate and capable of causing disasters as well as bringing good luck to people, and sacrificial rites of various kinds must be performed to appease them (Zhang 2000). Of all the deities that populate the world the three most important are the Supreme deities: Igu Ake, the first great cause, Saluwete, the biggest heavenly god; and Heduwapa, the great god of White Bones. In a secondary level are the Yuma protector deities, usually depicted as birds, the warrior deities, wisdom deities, deities of grains and domestic animals, ancestral gods, deities of benevolence and family gods (Guo 1991).

Igu Ake is the first great cause and takes first place in Naxi pantheon. No paintings exist of him and his name is always written with the Tibetan letter A. His evil counterpart is Igu Tina, who is usually represented by the Tibetan letter Na (Rock: 1972: 17). His origin is narrated in one myth: "Reality and unreality came forth, also competency and incompetency, reality and competency caused a magic and there came forth a brilliant blue object, and this caused a magic and there came forth something like a man who had a fine voice and fine breath, this caused a magic and there came forth Igu Ake. In the beginning Igu Ake caused a magic and there came forth a white egg and from the latter was born a white chicken that could neither fly nor dance, it laid nine pairs of white eggs that were the origin of all what exists in the world". Igu Ake also caused a magic and there came forth Saluwete, and from him Muanlluddundzi, the first ancestor, was created, he also caused a magic and came forth a white heaven, white land, white sun, etc. (Rock 1952: 676, 694).

Saluwete (Soyiwade) is the second great god of the Naxi. He is considered the chief of the gods and reposes in a lotus throne supported by lions. In some texts he precedes Igu Ake, who only became a reality after Saluwete meditated on him. Heduwapa (Haddu Oper) is the great god of the white bones; represented with a white body in the attitude of meditation, his halo surrounded by clouds. He wears a large cape, a necklace and a diadem of jewels. He rests on a lotus throne supported by cranes. On his shoulders is a Dharma wheel, and near him usually is placed a mystic jewel. He is usually surrounded by minor deities. Images of these two gods are heavily influenced by Buddhist iconography (Rock 1972).

Muanlluddundzi is the first ancestor, usually painted with a high forehead and a long white beard and accompanied by a crane and a deer as the Chinese God of Longevity. His victory over the black demons in *The War between Black and White* is the start of human conscience (Rock 1972). Congrenlien is the first post-flood ancestor. His marriage with the celestial princess Cunhongbaobai gave origin to human beings (Tibetan, Bai and Naxi). He is continuously referred to in their mythology, with his experiences molding the future culture of the Naxi. Omaha is the god of the grain. He dwells on the grain rack. The symbol "vagina" is used phonetically in his name. He has five daughters, which suggests that each daughter governs one kind of grain. The Shizhi are Mountain spirits (Rock 1972: 87).

Among the domestic deities, the Sv life god is of paramount importance. He protects the family taking care of each of its members. Old men in a family are also called *sv*. When an old man dies, people speak of him as a *sv mun* or Sv life god dead. *Sv-bbu* is a paternal ancestor for whom the Khinv funerary ceremony has not been performed. After it he is called *sv-bbu yu* or ancestor. T'alazomunnun is the god of the hearth. The Sv life god of the husband and that of the wife are tied with a cord to the hearth god; the cord is also tied to a newly married couple at wedding, and to the basket where the Sv god resides. The 18 Non spirits worshipped at home protect domestic animals (Rock 1952: 250, 411, 450; Rock 1972: 43).

Some goddesses (*Hami* in their language) play also a main role in their religious thought. Among them Ama Gkyimawut'su is the great goddess; the mother of Igu Ake, to whose realm the dead are escorted. Gkodzidtulluma is a

101

personal goddess which protects the people, commonly depicted riding a red tiger. Pangzusamei is the goddess which distributed the books of divination. T'a-yi la-mun is a celestial goddess that brewed the first liquor from white rice, white wheat and barley. The resulting white liquor was used in performing Ch'ung-bpa ba. Ts'uchwua gyimun, the wife of Muanlluddundzi, is considered the mother of the people, as he is the father. They cause children to be born and the grain to grow and ripen. They had nine sons and nine daughters (Rock 1972: 45- 58).

Garuda birds, Derko and Yuma are protective tutelary spirits. There are 360 of each kind, with Derko taking precedence over the Yuma. They have a bird body and head of different animals. They play an important role in the main Naxi rituals, which are constructed around snake deities, bird deities and the myth of the fight between snakes and birds. Among the snake deities the most important are the Shu nature spirits, the dragon related with water and the Shizhi snakes that posses every geographical accident. The central mythic theme of the fight between the Garuda and the snake, symbolically enacted during the most important Naxi ceremonies to reestablish the equilibrium between Shu and human beings, is common to the Naxi, Tibetan and Indian traditions (Zamblera). The fight between snake and eagle could be a symbol of the contradictions at the inner personal level between body and soul or between the terrestrial enchainment of the body and the celestial liberation of the soul. The equilibrium reestablished thanks to the Dongba ceremony would correspond to the inner peace usually attributed to the

Main deities of the Naxi, from left to right: Iku Ake, the supreme god, Shu spirits of nature, Sanduo protector god of Lijiang, Sv life god (represented as the Sv basket), Dongba Shiluo, ancestor of the Dongbas, Yuma and Derko protector, with shape of birds, Omaha god of grain, Non spirits, protector of domestic animals, and Der

intervention of priest and shamans that settle inner human contradictions.

Dongba Demons

The Naxi believe in the existence of malignant spirits or demons that can cause troubles or misfortune to human beings. There are two main kinds of demons: Nature demons and human demons. Each of the problems that can happen during a person existence can be attributed to a particular demon. That is, if the grains don't ripen and the ears are empty, this is believed to be caused by the Gkv-ts'u demons; if the people see ghosts and often quarrel, this is so because the Khyu and O demons; quarrels between married people are caused however by the Na-dtv-ts'u demons who dwell in caves;

if the fields are covered by rocks or sand, is caused by the Lv ts'u; if people have bad dreams during the night, bones or flesh are aching, is caused by the Mbe-ts'u demons who liberate disease. Boils and leprosy are caused by the Gkyi demons, and the pain that accompanies the disease, by the Tkhyi demons; fire, by the Mi demons able to fly; dropsy, by the Mbu ts'u demons, etc. Other problems are caused by Ghugh and Mun water demons, the snake demons of illness or the demons of laziness. Epidemics in cattle are caused by the Nder ts'u demons, curiously considered to be tiny worms (Rock 1972: 292).

These malignant and destructive demons, who plagued mankind with their malicious interference are pictured in Naxi manuscripts with a human head, a snake body and a repulsive appearance. They "ensconced themselves in the households, where disharmony occurred, and tugged telepathically at the disordered thoughts of the miserable or the depressed, inciting in them the ideas of revenge, murder or suicide" (Goullart 1957: 235). Most demons originated as a product of the sinful behavior of a person, usually called the mother of this kind of demons. They could be considered manifestations of the defects of the person, reflection of his bad situations. Their negative interference in human lives is the negative part of the human soul, as is shown with the Lachou demons of impurity, the personified sins of a deceased person, that close his soul's road to the ancestors' realm. Their human origins are told in their myths, as the Dter ts'u or headless demons, who are the transformation of the soul of any person dying unattended, killed by falling rocks or trees, by lightning, in battle, devoured by wild animals, etc., or the Gkyi ts'u cloud demons, which were originally females who, in the dim past, committed suicide. Za ts'u demons are related also with suicide; they dwell on trees on which the suicides are induced to hang themselves and devour the bodies of suicides on the mountains, the Ddv demons ride black horses and cause people to strangle themselves, the Yu ts'u or demons of suicide, are the spirits of persons who having committed suicide, entice other people to commit suicide[12] (Rock 1972: 261-319). When someone is killed in a house or a woman dies there in childbirth, the place automatically becomes unclean. The Dongbas are then invited to perform a purification ceremony in which the demons of uncleanness and calamity are convened, feasted and driven out (Goullart 1957: 258).

The belief that after death the human soul can be transformed into a god or a devil is common to a great part of East Asia. Among the Han Chinese, those dead souls would become *shen* (spirits generally benign) or *gui* (malignant spirits or devils) that can harm people, depending on the after death care provided by their relatives (Feuchtwang 2001). Among the Yi there is also the idea that the soul of the dead can become a *ne* spirit, a powerful spiritual entity that can harm people; they also differentiate between the proper and improper death (Vanicelli 1944). The Hani also think that "a person dying a bad death may become a spirit" (Lewis and Bai 2002: 124). The Jingpo believe that every soul becomes a "spirit at death and should be sent off to the "old homeland", and that those who refuse to go there cause trouble for their living family members (Wang Zhusheng 1997: 174). Similar ideas are found among other peoples that speak languages related with the

---

[12] A belief also found among the Chinese.

105

Naxi, and even in the farther north of China: "Some of the ancestors of the Tungus-speaking groups could be dangerous to the living if their souls were unable to reach the next world; or they could become demons or ghosts" (Stutley 2002: 101).

Dongba ritual books

To mediate between men and the multitude of spirits that can harm them; and to harness these spirits Dongba priests perform different ceremonies guided by their scriptures. There are 1,000 kinds of Dongba scriptures in more than 20,000 volumes preserved in libraries around the world: An encyclopedia of ancient Naxi wisdom and culture with contents including religion, history, social life, language, philosophy, folklore, literature, astronomy, geography, medicine, mythology, art, science and technology, etc. The extension of the Dongba manuscripts to include matters beyond the scope of the religious affairs, is due to the need to always relate the origin of any particular being the book deals with, because, unless his origin is related, he cannot be invited, beseeched, or suppressed (Rock 1937: 3; Zhang Tongsheng 2001: 104).

Dongba scriptures were written in pictographs which consist of some hundreds of human and animal drawings, figures of demons, gods and priests, parts of human and animal bodies, insects and plants, natural phenomena, landscapes, tools, weapons, foods, clothing, religious paraphernalia, etc. The main purpose of writing down the ritual texts was to be able to pick out the key elements so that they would be chanted in the correct order. Such a system is more like a restricted code than a true written language and, indeed, its function was simply to act as a mnemonic device to jog the Dongba's memory as he chanted by heart, as most of the Dongba know by memory the text of the ceremonies, learned during their long apprenticeship years (Pan 1998: 275).

A pictographic manuscript typically consists of about thirty to forty pages, which are about twenty-eight centimeters in width to nine centimeters in height, held together by a string on the left-hand side. One such booklet contains a ritual text, one of more than a hundred texts usually needed for some of the longest ceremonies. The basic kinds of books used in the Dongba ceremonies are divination books, index books and ritual books. Prayers for blessings and *dharanis* or charms to exorcise demons constitute also an important part of their scriptures (Jackson and Pan 1998: 240).

Every ceremony possesses an index book in which the names of the books to be chanted are given in the prescribed order, the ritual objects that will be used, the arrangements of the ritual space, the paraphernalia used, the animals to be sacrificed, number of tress, gates for the gods and demons, etc.; all is enumerated. The index books provide important information that allows the reader to recreate the general course of a ceremony. The number of books to be chanted varies considerably, and depends of the number of books the Dongba possesses; the sequence is often different. In Dongba outdoor rituals the portraits of gods for worshiping and ghosts to be drive out are painted on wooden slabs and planted in the sacrificial spot. When the ritual is over, wooden-slabs of gods could be taken back home and worshipped while the slabs of ghosts have to be destroyed on the spot (He and He 1999: 47; Jackson and Pan 1998: 255; Rock 1963: 633).

Divination in Dongba religion

Divination plays a major role in Dongba religion. The books of divination, called Dso-la, are of paramount importance; without them only Worship to Heaven and routine ceremonies for the increase of herds or crops could be performed because the books of divination provide information about the origin of the problem, that is, about the nature of the demon involved, and they outline procedures to solve it, which mostly comprise the performance of a ceremony (Rock 1952: 655). These books are compilations recording the results of divination by different techniques, which can be divided in time-based divination, which concerns childbirth, marriage, illness and death, and chance-based divination, which concerns the welfare of children, illness, and fortune and misfortune in everyday activities (Jackson and Pan 1998: 250). The resurgence of Dongba activities in the last years has had divination as the main protagonist. Dongbas are asked to divine after a new birth, to choose a proper name to the new born, before a wedding to know if the union will be happy, before starting a long travel or a new business, to choose the proper place and time to lift a new house, if somebody lost something, if the cattle did not multiply, etc.; with Dongba choosing the technique that he considers more suitable to every case.

There are more than ten main ways of divination, some of them relate the Naxi to the dawn of civilization in East Asia, as one of the oldest divination techniques used in China is preserved among them: The reading of the cracks appearing after burning the periosteum of a mutton shoulder blade, a variant of the divination that was in use in the Chinese Shang dynasty more than 3.000 years ago (Rock 1963: 102). Little tinder is pasted on the flat side of a sheep shoulder-blade and then lighted; the resulting cracks are examined and interpreted with the help of a book in which the shape of the various possible fissures of the bone are explained (Rock 1963). The importance of this divination method can be perceived knowing that the name of the shoulder blade (p'i), also mean to decide, judge, verdict (Rock 1963: 377).

Calendar divination is based on the horoscope of a person and the days of the lunar month. It is useful to determine which days will be auspicious to perform which activities and which days will not. To divine by the horoscope, the Dongba will search in a book which contains information about the auspiciousness of different situations. The first section, with information related with the 12 signs of the zodiac, will provide a general assessment of the problem: "If the person is sick the sickness will not follow a good healing, if there is a fire, it will be dangerous, there are demons around. Man and woman have no strength. Animals can die". The next section contains the 30 days of the month. Reading it the Dongba tries to specify the curse the problem will follows. The third part contains instructions to avoid further problems.

Very similar to the *I Ching* of Chinese culture is the shell-throwing divination, when two cowrie shells flattened and blackened on one side are thrown thrice and the result interpreted in a Dongba book that contents all possible combinations. Sometimes five shells are thrown twice and the result interpreted. In the divination by the Naxi Tarot 32 finely painted cards are used. Each card has a drawing in the upper side, a text related to the drawing below and in the back, and a string attached to his upper side. Before divination, all cards are mixed and the person who wants his luck divined must select one of these strings attached to one card. The Dongba will help him to take it out with the card, and will read and interpret the advices printed in it. The card of the Zhasanapu, a mythical being with a dragon's head and a tail, is not auspicious: "In the village thunders could fall, fight with enemies would be full of dangers. Bad demons can cause problems. It is better not travel too far, because there is the danger of being lost. A roving demon must be expelled and the soul must be called back to the body. Still there are bad things lurking, with enemies fighting. If the soul of the sick person is recovered there can be safety, if is not possible, there will be many problems."

Bage chart or frog divination is equivalent to the Chinese *bagua*. It is called frog divination because a yellow frog, drawn in a circular piece of paper, is placed in the center of the chart. The head, tail, four legs and abdomen of the frog separately represent the five directions. Around them are added into the chart the twelve animals of the year. To divine the good or bad luck and the result for illness or marriage of the people, the Dongba throws a needle into the chart and he interprets by means of a book the direction the needle points. According to their legends after the golden frog had been shot, its head pointed south (left) and its tail north (right). The tail changed into the eastern wood element, its blood into the fire element in the south, its bones into the metal element in the west, its bile into the water element in the north, and its flesh into the earth element in the center. The frog's four legs changed into the four subcardinal regions between heaven and earth (Rock 1963: 28, 161; Li Xi and A Yuan 1998: 58).

In time or finger divination, "units of time are calculated on the fingers to reveal one's fate. The divination is carried out by counting along six points (corresponding to the three bones on each finger) on the index and middle fingers according to the time – the month, the day or the hour – that the petitioner asks the Dongba to conduct the divination, and the Dongba consults the reading for the particular point where he stops counting." An auspicious result would be: "a hundred thousand things are all propitious, searching for gold and silver will also have favourable results. If valuables have been lost, they have not gone far. There will be no quarrels. If a long journey is made, nothing will befall the traveler. Someone in the family will fall ill. If one goes to act as a headman, they will be transferred home" (Duncan 2010b).

Chicken black stripes is a type of horoscope during which the bones of a black chicken are boiled, and the appearing stripes on the periosteum of the bone are interpreted (Rock 1963: 3). String divination is one of the oldest kinds of horoscopes. Nine strings are rolled between the palms of the hands. Holding them before his face, the Dongba blows on them and meditated on the affair about which he is desirous of enlightenment. Later both ends of each string are tied together with the eyes closed, and rolled first on the left side of his body, then on the right, in the back and in the front, thence once more rolled between his hands in front of his face and then dropped on the table, and the position of the strings interpreted (Rock 1963: 283). They also can divine looking at

111

the stars, watching the earth, calculating the four cardinal points, etc.

Dongba ceremonies

The ritual activities of the Dongba range from magnificent rites performed in honor of the sky, the earth and the gods to those performed for wholly domestic matters such as weddings, funerals, expiating the sins of the dead and curing diseases (Zhang 2000). Naxi ritual ceremonies can be divided into two kinds: rituals that accompany the normal development of life, including rites related with the production cycle and funerals, conducted in the past by lineage heads; and rites concerning abnormal situations, including sickness, misfortune and other disasters, formerly performed by shamans. Over this structure, the first Dongba superimposed the cult of their founder Dongba Shiluo to mediate between people and demons (Jackson 1978). The function of the rituals varies according to whether they belong to the production cycle of the agricultural year or to the individual life cycle. A distinguishing feature of the production cycle rites is that they take place away from the villages, are performed by groups of related families and do not necessitate the services of a Dongba. Life cycle ceremonies are contingent upon birth, marriage, illness, misfortune and death and hence are more haphazard in the occurrence; they are more complicated and diversified and are performed, on demand, by Dongbas (Jackson 1979: 107). Most of the Dongba ceremonies are performed after unexpected events that can happen during the life of a person; the biggest ceremonies were developed to solve situations happening frequently, while strange events

112

Divination in Dongba religion, from left to right: sheep blade divination, Dsola books divination, shell divination and frog divination.

rarely happen are responded to with shorter ceremonies. Many ceremonies are related to death, a dangerous moment that can produce the birth of new demons (Rock 1937: 40).

There are over 100 ceremonies, 1,000 rites, 2,000 different deities and 10,000 texts, but despite the apparently enormous number of ritual texts, the average ceremony is quite short, with the actual working library of a Dongba not exceeding probably a couple of hundred texts. The most important ceremonies last several days and require the chanting of over 100 books; all of them are the integration of Dongba texts, painting, utensils, music, dance and art. Without standardized ceremonies the Dongba were relatively free to compose their rites within the guidelines set down by precedent, symbolic usage and general custom, taking its components from certain sub ceremonies which formed a basic core of material common to the rituals as a whole (Jackson 1979: 22, 26, 174).

Dongba ceremonies address the contradictory relationship between man and nature and man and society (Li Ji and A Yuan 1998: 16). The most important are the sacrifices

113

to heaven, wind, dragon, and to the god of longevity. Joseph Rock classified them into fifteen types: worship of nature, of wind and mountain spirits, of Shu serpent spirits, prayers for the prosperity of the family and the increase of flocks, propitiation, purification and cleaning of a place, funerary (including to open the road to the souls, and to end the funeral) and marriage ceremonies, inviting the ancestors, prolongation of life, prevention of evil arising from the sky and land, to avoid calamities, propitiation and eviction of demons, elimination of accumulated sins, suicides and unnatural deaths. There were seven ceremonies performed by the *llubhu* (Goodman 1997: 120 and He Zhiwu 1989).

A Dongba ceremony can be divided in several stages that are performed in a fixed order, the central one being the acquisition of power. All ceremonies start with the preparations and cleansing of the place, which, being the scene of a recent misfortune will be impure or polluted by demons, which must be expelled before beginning. Second is the invitation to the deities and spirits to descend. The gods that should be invited are indicated with their paintings. More than 20 great gods have special portraits, while minor deities encircle the main gods (He and He 1999: 41). With their help the Dongba can conquer various ghosts and evict the demons who might spoil the ceremony. Then gods and Shu spirits are called from their respective realms. The sacrifice marks the moment when offerings are done to the gods or the debt incurred in by the humans is repaid to the Shu. The request for power is the most important part of the ceremony. The Dongba gets the mediating power between human and gods that Dongba Shiluo possessed in mythical times. With his recently acquired power, the Dongba can expel the evil spirits that caused the problem or those that can cause a problem in the future. To achieve its object each rite must be effective, and effectiveness is remembered and assured to the sick person through the recitation of its past usage: This means to chant the story of its origin sometimes followed by a monotonous repetition of

Cards of the Naxi tarot ritually used by Dongba He Zhiben

stories of similar content that emphasize the effectiveness of the ritual. Once the aim of the ceremony has been reached, the ceremonial site must be dismantled, closing the ceremonial ground and removing trees and paintings. At the end all the gods and Shu nature spirits that were invoked to attend are escorted to their respective realms (Jackson 1979: 207, 209).

The ceremonial articles comprise white conchs, yak horns, flat metal cymbals, large hide-covered drums, small twirling hand drums, double sided hand drums, brass gongs, broadswords, sickles, bows and arrows (He and He 1998: 141). "Dongba rituals take place in dedicated and occasional spaces within the village, in fields, near natural springs or in people's houses" (Rubin 2011: 2). They use three types of altars. The first is merely a Chinese table set up in the open porch of a farmhouse or in an unused room with a cubical lantern of coloured paper in the center and a butter lamp inside it. "Behind the light is the replica of a ploughshare made of lead, over its point is draped a string of white beads", a symbol of the sacred Junaruoluo (Sumeru) mountain among the clouds. On the table, at either side of the light stand a pair of paper pennants, triangular in shape and perforated in geometrical patterns, and behind these the paintings depicting the main deities are hanged. Around are grouped the ceremonial objects that the priests will use: the cymbal, the drum, the gong, the holy books, and a pair of ordinary cups holding simple vegetable offerings (Roosevelt 7). The altar will be presided by some *thangka* paintings depicting Dongba Shiluo and other deities, and some Yuma celestial guardians.

Ceremony to Propitiate the Demons of Suicide (Harlalluko)

Harlalluko is the ceremony performed for the propitiation of demons of suicide by hanging, poisoning, or drowning, committed either singly or by couples. It is one of the most elaborated and costly ceremonies, and the largest ritual of the Naxi. From the making of the ceremonial articles to the conclusion of the sacrificial rite, a period of five successive days is required (He and He 1998). It needs at least

116

three to five Dongbas chanting in sequence one hundred and twenty books, and the making of over ninety wooden slats; the sacrifice of two fattened pigs, two sheep, two goats and six chickens. Friends and relatives from the locality must be invited to participate and 150 kilos of grain are consumed. It is believed that a person becomes a wind demon if he is seduced by the Yuvu queens to commit suicide and thus fails to have the traditional grains of rice placed beneath his tongue before dying; without these grains his soul is transformed into evil or ferocious demons, wandering all over the earth, making trouble and stirring up mischief, causing people to fall sick and suffer disasters, menacing the development of livestock, harming the growth of crops, confusing the minds of people and especially enticing young people to the pernicious destruction by means of love suicide or violent death (He and He 1998: 139). The suicide of a person is an unlucky event for his relatives, in the aftermath of which illness and other calamities can strike them because the suicide's soul became a wind demon and through misfortune indicates his wish to join his ancestors (Jackson 1979: 51). The aim of perform *Harlalluku* ceremony is to turn the spirit from a wild demon into a soul that can be led to the realm of his ancestors.

The ceremony begins in the courtyard and ends outside the village where all the ritual paraphernalia is re-erected. The main altar consists of a long bench upon which are placed seven dolls representing the first seven girl-suicides among the Naxi, and facing them are 13 k'o-byo representing the 13 Yuvu queens, the enticers of suicide (Jackson 1979:138). Special *Harlalluko* ceremonies are performed for people that die strange deaths. Common deaths are dealt with the standard funeral

117

rite, the Zhima ceremony, whose main aim is to show the road to the ancestor's lands.

To close the gate of the dead (Shi Ku Dter Bpo) is a ceremony performed to prevent members of a family to die successively. It is believed that after the decease of a person other members of the family can successively die, being the first responsible for calling the others to follow. With this ceremony the gate of the dead is closed (Rock 1972: 405).

Rite for prolongation of life (Szi Chung bpo) is performed after a funeral for the benefit of the survivors, because it is though that the death which precedes the holding of this rite has caused a break in the chain of life, thus hazarding the life expectancy of the survivors; the ceremony aims at restoring their lost longevity, as the Sv life god has withdrawn his presence and protection. All men are thought to have guardian spirits that play an important role in this ceremony of restoring longevity. The thirteen Swastica goddesses which prevent human demons from stealing longevity are worshipped (Rock 1972: 497; Jackson: 1979: 184).

Ceremony for purification (Chou na gv) of either a place or a house. The night before the performance of a larger rite the site must be purified of impurity, for, unless this is done the invoked deities will refuse to attend. In an improvised chapel three painted scrolls are hung behind the centre altar: they depict Dongba Shiluo flanked by two Yuma deities (Jackson 1979: 119).

The ceremony of a scapegoat to avert calamities (Dto Na Ko) is the only instance of a ceremony using a human sacrifice, generally slaves purchased from other places to be

118

used in this ritual. The sacrificial victim was not killed but was made a scapegoat, heaping upon him all the curses, calamities, and evils of the past, thus freeing the country of all its evils. Then he would be given presents and a horse and was sent out into the wilderness and left there to his or her fate, and never permitted to return. He was dead within a week. People considered that this scapegoat could take away all past, present and future disasters and calamities from the household, the village or the entire region (Yang 1998: 204; Rock 1972: 388)

Other interesting Dongba rituals are the Propitiation of the Non, the protectors of domestic animals. A ceremony performed on an alpine meadow to propitiate the mountain's spirits in order to protect the sheep from being lost or eaten by wild animals. No sacrifice is made in this ceremony but instead an animal is dedicated to the spirits, it is set free and can neither be killed nor sold (Jackson 1979: 113).

Ceremonies to call the soul can be performed for the living people or for the dead. To know the reason of the loss of the soul a Dongba who would recur to divination or a *llubhu* would go directly in search of the soul. They believe that sometimes is hunger the reason for the soul to leave the body, as well as the wish to live again in the freedom of natural life, out of the constraints of civilization, as many prayers ask the roving soul not to eat the food of the Shu spirits, fearing that if the soul eat again the food of the natural life it would not want to come back to the body. In abnormal death ceremonies the calling of the soul is also performed, the circumstances of the dead are investigated and a chicken is killed to substitute the body (Bai 2001: 91).

Some Dongba demons, from left to right: Demon, demon of fire, hungry demon, with a big belly with nothing inside, demon of pestilence, with a shit in his hand, Zee demon, headless demon, result of the people killed; tiger demon, result of the people who die attacked by wild animals, bbee demon of infertility, discharges from the vagina are seen, woman demon, suicide demon, and love demon.

Minor ceremonies responded to events that, though not recurrent in everyday life, were quite common in Naxi existence. As they believed that demons were responsible for bad luck and calamities, ceremonies had to be performed to reestablish the spiritual equilibrium. A careful reading of these small ceremonies would show a correspondence with the demons that had to be suppresses or driven out. As Mi-ko demons were responsible for sins of omission, *Mi-ko bpo* ceremony is performed for divesting oneself of sin, after a task during which a sin of omission may have been incurred. As Mi are demons of fire, the ceremony for the suppression of the Mi fire demons (*Mi szer bpo*) is performed after a fire occurs in a house, to prevent a larger fire to occur. A miniature house is made, and fire demons are placed on each side, then the house is set on fire and the fire extinguished with five bowls of water from the Yangtze River. As Mun and Ghugh are demons of water, a ceremony to propitiate them (*Mun ghugh bpo*) is performed after people have drowned themselves, when the soul must be redeemed from these spirits, and they must be repaid with a chicken. When there is an epidemic among the cattle *Nder ts'u tu bpo*, or ceremony to drive out the Ndter demons that cause epidemics must be performed. Other ceremonies are performed if anyone is killed in a fight (*O-per O na bpo*), if a woman married two or three years has not given birth to children (*O-la-nnu*), when a false pregnancy occurs (*Ts'u bpo*), when a male child is not able to speak although he is already several years old (*Zo khi ko bpo-lu bpo*), when somebody becomes suddenly unconscious, etc. *Ti-lua ts'u to bpo* or ceremony to drive out the Ti-lua demons is performed when a family's home is bombarded with rocks, or a fire has destroyed the home. *To-lo ts'u to bpo* is the ceremony to drive out the To-lo demons, performed if a family dies out and other people (distant relatives) take possession of the house and property, and in the course of time illness should visit the new occupants, which is attributed to the previous, deceased owners, turned demons. *Tu lvlv bpo* or ceremony to propitiate the nine Tu or earth and rock demons, is performed when building a house or moving a box. At this ceremony, a round hole is dug in the court of the house and is thought that its soul has been freed. Two *duoma* are placed into the hole and the soul is redeemed and recalled. *Zhi ts'u bpo* or ceremony to escort the snake-

121

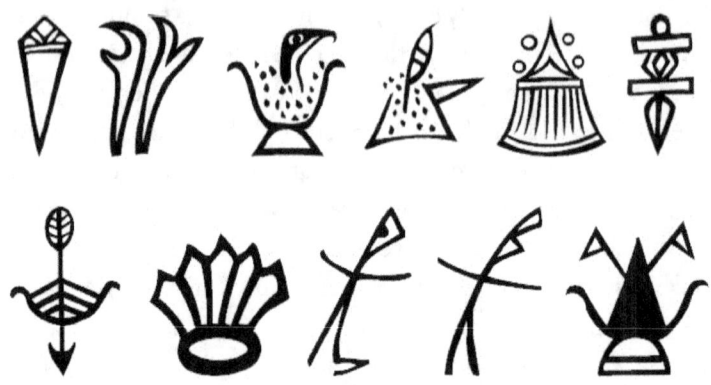

Some ritual implements of the Dongba shamans. From left to right: Wooden slabs, sacrificial puppet, sacrificial rice, sacrificial lamb, altar, vajra ceremonial knife of Tibetan origin, ceremonial arrow, five lobes crown, two kinds of wooden figurines, duoma sculpture.

demons is performed when it is believed that these demons have made a person ill. *Zo mi bpo* or ceremony for a boy or girl is performed at the birth of a child to prevent demons from doing harm to him (Rock 1972: 424-443).

There are also some short ceremonies performed in a preventive way, as the *Dsu bpo* ceremony, when the spirit of conception and copulation (Dsu) is beseeched to grant long life and offspring, the *Ffu-dtv bpo* ceremony for the benefit of all animals having blood, the *Gkan-ds shu bpo* or worshiping the local spirits or land owners. *Gyi-ko bpo* or water spring ceremony is performed on the first day of the year, when one man from each family rises at dawn and betakes himself to the nearest spring to propitiate the Llu-mun, and beseech them for long life and riches. *Ha la bpo* or ceremony to strike the soul, performed when the soul of a person is to be killed. In *Ho bpo*, or semen ceremony, the spirit of the male semen *ho*, is beseeched for offspring, long life, and proper ejaculation. In *Khi ka dzu pu ha bpo* ceremony the soul of the deceased is called by the relatives, sons and daughters. *Llu bpo* is the ceremony for propitiating the spirit of the hunt, performed before a party goes on a hunting expedition. *Mbbue bpo* or ceremony to propitiate the Mbbue demons is performed if the male members of the family have all died and there is no one to inherit the property as females cannot inherit. People who buy such property perform this ceremony before taking possession of it; for fear that they too will die out. To do it, they set aside a small worthless field on which they pile old agricultural implements and household goods for the spirits of the defunct family. *Ngaw bpo* or ceremony to propitiate the Ngaw, is performed only in the presence of men after the birth of a child, when Heaven, Earth and the constellation of 28 stars are worshipped, and beseeched to grant him long life. *Non bbu bpu* is a ceremony to beseech the Non (protectors of all domestic animals) for abundant riches, fertility, victory over the enemy, courage, agility, long life and sufficient food. *Omaha bpo* is the ceremony to worship Omaha the god of grain. *Za bbu bpo* is a ceremony for increasing or protecting the flocks, a rite for females only, for all offered animals, either chickens or pigs must be females. The ceremony to escort the leopard and tiger demons (*Sher ts'u la ts'u bpu*), female demons that only take possession of women, and made any person so possessed able to give illness to people and cause death to children, requires gold and silver to be placed on the open road in sufficient quantities to entice the greedy demons to leave the particular person, and to discard a good female dress (Rock 1972: 424-443).

What transcends in the above descriptions is that any unexpected event doing any harm to one person, his family, house, flock or crops, is believed to be caused by a demon; a spirit that can be driven out or appeased with the corresponding ceremony. As most of these problems are caused by demons born as a result of improper care at the time of death, Zhima ceremony is the main funeral performed for all, irrespective of rank or sex, to prevent the creation of new demons. Persons of rank enjoy especial funerals. In the funeral for a Dongba, his son receives the *ds-ler* from the hand of the leading Dongba officiating at the funeral, and he is invested with other ceremonial articles and the sword with which his father fought the demons. Wives of Dongbas have a special funeral. D'a nv is the funeral for a courageous warrior; anyone who vanquished his enemy, killed him, or was in any way renowned. For a courageous woman Mbbue D'a nv funeral is performed. Szi-sher ddu nv is the funeral for long living men. Dter nv is the funeral for a Dter head-less demon, a person who died unattended, usually by accident. Mi-lv dzu nv is the funeral for a married couple who died at the same time, considered very unlucky. The care taken in dealing with the different kinds of deaths shows that death is a dangerous moment in which the deceased soul could become a demon and the Dongba must act to prevent it.

Ceremony to the Shu nature spirits

To understand the performance of a Naxi ceremony we will sail across the sea of information provided in the monumental book of Joseph Rock, the *Nakhi Naga Cults and Related Ceremonies*, where the *SSu ddu gv* or ceremony to the Shu[13] nature spirits is described, a ceremony that lasted three days and was performed by four Dongba priests.

The burning of hillsides or forests, the digging of ditches, the polluting of springs are all considered crimes against the Shu, which can turn their friendship in enmity, stealing men's souls which thereupon become ill. The Sv life god leaves the house, and there is a risk of dying unless the Shu are propitiated by the performance of the proper ceremonies. As these Shu spirits made the human being share the soul of nature, it means that any damage men cause on nature it is damage to them; and it is only logic that the part of the humans that is shared with nature, this Sv life god, could be taken away from them. The Dongba is believed to be able to force the Shu to release the souls they have stolen or imprisoned. Thus the ceremony is performed on one hand to repay them for the damage done, hunting wild animals, digging wells, cutting tress, mining silver, washing gold, fishing in the streams, setting fire to forests, etc., and at the same time to destroy their power by the intermediation of Dongba Shiluo and the Garuda bird.

The ceremony begins with the preparation and cleansing of the place of sacrifice, when the Ssu-ndo serpent demons, which are believed to be able to give illness to the people, are chased out by the Dongba ringing the *ds-ler* and brandishing a sword. As they can cause the people to fall ill

---

[13] Rock identifies them with the Nagas in the Sanskrit literature.

tying ropes to them, they must be repaid with a grain offering. Then the family transfers their illness sticking needles in a human *duoma* figure and expels it out of the house.

In the book *Invite the Garuda* all the disturbances that the Shu caused to the family are related, and the central role of Dongba Shiluo and the Garudas to repay or suppress the Shu spirits is remembered. If the power of the Garudas is not invoked and instances of their effectiveness provided, nobody will trust the effectiveness of this ritual. Then the origin of the five regional Garudas is related. In *Grain thrown out* the grain is thrown towards the banners depicting Naxi deities while hymns are chanted to them. The origin of this rite and former instances when the mythical ancestors performed it, is chanted. In the evening butter lamps are lighted before the banners, while a myth is chanted that describes how the ancestors of the Naxi asked their Dongbas to make butter lamps and to light them to the deities, and how all they got long life and numerous progeny. Then they chant a long prayer to the multitude of gods and deities to whom this family's lamps will be lighted. "To the power of the high heavens, and to the power of the vast lands, we offer this lamp; to the rays of sun and to the power of the moon..." At the end is repeated that this family is desirous of long life and numerous sons and daughters.

This is followed by the enumeration and description of all the Shu kings and queens, and smaller Shu ruling over individual mountains or valleys, as they are invited to descend and partake of the grain and precious objects prepared for them. All the Shu must be invited as the Dongba cannot know the domains of whom the family inadvertently trespassed. As a

126

way to ensure the validity of this ceremony some historical precedents are chanted; stories of people that inadvertently offended the Shu and felt sick, and with the help of Dongba Shiluo they repaid the Shu and get healed.

When all the elements of the ceremony are ready the Dongba must acquire power. Chanting *Yang principle rises* he exposes his own merit, reciting the way it has been acquired; chanting *Power Invest* he beseeches the gods, spirits, and deified Dongbas to invest him with their power, which will allow him to deal with malevolent spirits and demons.

The origin of medicine is chanted before various Shu images that are sprinkled with a liquid supposed to represent medicine, for no object may be used or talked about unless its origin is first related. The Dongba remembers the origin of medicine, and enumerates the Shu to whom the medicine will be given. "Let the family have no more illness, let the family be rich, let our ears hear only good tidings, let our ponds be full." To probe the usefulness of the medicine *Tso-dze-per-ddu search for medicine* is chanted. A nice tale that tells how the hero, finding his parents dead, leave in search of the medicine to revive them, but after found it, the demon who possessed it pursue him and by a magic make it spill; thanks to this spilling there is medicine everywhere: in heaven and earth, trees, plants, etc. The process of sprinkle medicine to the Shu with a juniper twig is materialized while chanting a manuscript that relates which kind of medicine must be used for each illness.

One of the most important myths of the Naxi is related here: The first human and the first Shu shared the same mother but had different fathers. Later they became enemies, and they separated their realms. The first ancestor trespassed to the Shu's

127

realm, became ill, and he healed after repaying the Shu -the action enacted in this ceremony. The mother of the Shu tells other story with the same content. Once and again the Dongba repeats these sacred stories about humans that encroached the Shu's realm, were punished, and with the help of a Dongba repaid to them and healed. As this is the aim of the ceremony, the repetition of one instance after another in which the procedure healed the sick, would assure the patient that the therapeutic method is the correct, as has been in the past.

The effective healing is done through the *duoma* figurines that get the sickness affecting the patient. First it is explained the origin of *duoma* and then the multitude of deities honored with them are related. All impurities, demons, and evil spirits which are believed to be present in the house, are chased out with the *duoma*. The landlord kneels before the table and prostrates himself, dropping popped grain on the *duoma*. These *duoma* are about six inches high, and are made of flour and vegetable oil or butter, after being thrown out they are quickly devoured by dogs or crows.

The *Fight between the Garuda and Shu* is the key book of this ceremony, as it explains the victory of the Garuda and Dongba Shiluo, and justifies the future victory of the Dongba against the illness. This myth relates again stories of human beings who trespassed the Shu realms, got sick, and how, thanks to the mediation of the Garuda and Shiluo and recovered their health. As a witness to the pact a juniper pagoda is erected. While the Dongba relates how some mythic and historic personages erected a juniper pagoda for the Shu to dwell, and they protected their families, a hole is made in the center of the juniper trunk, considered the heart of the pagoda, where the following objects are inserted: Five kinds of grains, strings of five different colors representing the five elements, a little silver, gold, a small piece of turquoise and red coral or cornelian.

A chicken is sacrificed to repay the Shu, which would acts as a substitute for ill person. The different parts of the chicken used to repay to different kinds of Shu are described. To use the chicken its history must be told, as well as that of its liturgical use, which includes an interesting relation of its body parts with the elements of the nature.

Before finishing a chant relates how Shiluo protects the family and no illness is admitted, and how he stopped the fighting of the Shu with the people. A very interesting section is the narration of the possible offenses to the Shu, a kind of list of commandments to the natural world, maybe archaic norms to protect the forest and mountains and allow for the conservation of nature for future generations. After it the Dongba opens the lock of the gate with a key. The Shu are escorted to their particular realms, and they are asked to grant the family long life, riches and fertility; all the *k'o-byo* and other paraphernalia are transported to a nearby spring and re-arranged, the gods that have been called during the ceremony are escorted back, and the ceremony ends.

As in other therapeutic methods common to the minorities of south China, here we find also the belief that the sickness was caused by the spirits of nature following a transgression of their territorial rights, as well as a continuous narration of historical instances when people healed in this way. The main novelty is the incorporation of Dongba Shiluo, the Garuda, and the Dongba as the mediators in the healing.

CHAPTER 4

Naxi
Culture

In ancient times the forefathers of the Naxi were nomads living without fixed settlements in the grasslands of Eastern Tibet. Their main activities must have been hunting and fishing, herding cattle and maybe a seasonal primitive agriculture. After their settlement around Lijiang, trade and the manufacture of bronze wares and leather articles became important among them. Agriculture is now their main economical activity; wheat, maize, rice (in the lowlands) and potatoes are their main crops. They herd cows, sheep and goats. Naxi horses are well known in the province and neighbouring areas. Their yearly productive cycle is invested of a sacrality that gives the Dongba an active role in its crucial moments.

The natural environment that the Naxi inhabit is characterized by the presence of high mountains, dense forests with an incredible variety of flora and fauna, and a network of rivers, lakes and streams. Mountains and valleys, forests and rivers are important sources of resources for their livelihood. Natural resources have been preserved along centuries thanks to a religion that stresses the respect to the spirits of nature, and to the concept that Shu nature gods and human beings are two brothers who are in charge of different domains. Man for domestic areas and Shu for wild ones. The conflicts that surged in *illo tempore* between men and nature are reenacted every year in a way that every Naxi knows that he must take care of nature, and make a reasonable use of the natural resources needed for his livelihood. To avoid a selfish interpretation of the concept of "reasonable use of the natural resources", many Naxi communities manage their resources with an Elders Committee that, among other tasks, must supervise the forest guardian and the crop guardian of the village. These two offices, basic to the preservation of nature, can be either elected by the people or appointed by the Elders Committee. If a villager wants to build a house and needs logs, first he must apply to the Elders Committee, which would then approve the amount of wood that can be cut under the supervision of the forest guardian (Yang 2004: 4).

The Naxi concept of the universe is based on a dualism that develops the Chinese theories of yin-yang. In their beliefs the most important objects of worship are the heaven and the earth, with grand rituals sacrificing to the heaven god (Mee) and to the earth goddess (Dda). In their pictographic manuscripts and oral traditions, it is said that the heaven was made by male spirits and the earth by female ones. The concept of the earth as a mother stresses the close relation between female and the earthly natural resources. In Naxi legends, a lot of spirits of mountains, forests and meadows are female, as is the Love goddess, who rules a spiritual mountainous paradise for the people who committed love-pact suicide, or Meinabu, considered the mother of all Shu and Ni spirits of nature. There is a relationship between the female, mother earth and

131

Some activities of the Naxi, from left to right: herding, hunting (with dog), building (a man carries stones to put on the earth), forging (a smith hitting a piece of iron), rowing, and weaving.

the Shu spirits of nature that control all the earthly resources (Yang 1998). Shu and humans are brothers and at the same time they are a couple. The Shu are the daughters of the Mother Nature, the heiresses and administrators of her riches. In their double role of guardians and administrators they can punish those humans that trespass the mother domains as well as provide fertility and riches to the human beings. Human beings as a whole are considered males, sterile without the fertility of the female. The third duality implicit in the relationship between Shu and humans, already previously noted, is that while human beings have within their own share of the spirit of nature, their cultural activities are born of the contradictory need to destroy, at least in some grade, nature.

The human realm: Villages

Villages are usually sited alongside a stream or a spring, following a plan that reflects a radial division of space. A village typically consists of a cluster of 10-30 family compounds, each of which is comprised of two or more buildings facing onto a central courtyard. Their domestic realm is also aligned along the yin-yang concept and gender roles. The center, the domestic sphere, is generally regarded as female and agricultural, and the periphery as male and pastoral (McKhann 1989: 160). The women's territory comprises the house and the vegetable gardens, which give way to fields of grain and other staple crops. There they cook, clean the house, take care of the children, weave their textiles, and tend the family garden. Beyond these are the hillsides, forests and meadows where the Naxi grazes their livestock, hunt, gather firewood and wild plants for food and medicine, and cut timber for buildings; the territory of men. Boundaries between territories are not strictly fixed; women usually go outside the village for the gathering of wild plants and firewood or to the local markets.

Between the domesticated lands of the village and the savage wilderness of nature, there is a series of places of special religious significance which creates a sacred geography that separates and protects the human beings from the forces of nature. In Mingying Township, Dongba He Jihua signaled perfectly differentiated: The altar for Worshiping Heaven, the place to Worship Shu spirits, to worship wind, dragon, the god that protects peace and harmony, earth, and the god that protects against hailstorm; beyond, far in the mountains, there is the cremation place, the burying place (usually temporal) and the cave where the wood carvings made during the funeral are kept. Being the village at the foot of a small hill, it is interesting to remark that some of these sacred places are in a small forest above the village, a forest whose trees cannot be cut, which can protect the villagers from torrential rains and other natural disasters. This concept is common to many ethnic groups in Yunnan province, where sacred forests play a crucial role protecting the environment around the village, as reservoirs of natural resources contribute to avoid torrential floods, to preserve the soil and humidity, regulate temperature and increase the biodiversity (Gao 2000).

The spiritual protection of the village is in charge of the Village God, that together with the spirit of the mountain and the spirits of the ancestors who in the past lived in the village, are worshipped on the first or the seventh month, in a mountain above the village, where a simple altar is erected, to beseech peace and fortune. After the ritual cleansing of the place, the Dongba call to the village deities to descend and offer them a chicken chanting the sacred books: *To receive the God of the Village, To erect a sacrificial altar, To liberate a chicken to the God of the Village.* While the Dongba is chanting he expels with his sword the bad spirits of the place (Eroc: 402).

Above all Naxi villages stands Lijiang City, originally a cluster of villages at the foot of the Lion Mountain that was the capital during most of the Mu family kings rule and the seat of the Chinese administrations. One of the most charismatic urban habitats in Asia, the city forms an unique scenery, with the Square Street, the old marketplace that in the past concentrated trading activities, in the center, and a network of streets and channels with houses built on level upon level on hills, without uniform height. Lijiang is defined by mountains and water. Besides the small hills that surround the city, the Jade Dragon Mountain, with its imposing ever-snowed peaks, is visible from every house and street of Lijiang. Water arrives from the snow mountain. Divided in dozens of channels, it is present in most of Lijiang homes. The history of the city construction can be linked to the development of the water

Naxi agricultural cycle as seen in Dongba pictographs, from left to right: To do, a man with a hoe; to cut the trees, a man with an axe hit a tree; burnt the trees, a man with fire in his hand burn a tree; plough the land, drawing of a plough; dibble in seeds, sow seed s, pull up weeds, to winnow, to sun dry the grains, and to carry.

channels that provide water to the residents; with three main channels marking the construction of its three main parts. One of the most special water works in Lijiang is the system of three pools. The first of which is used to get drinking water, the second to wash the vegetables, and the third to wash clothes. Hundreds of small bridges of different styles and materials provide the ever changing urban perspectives that mark the character of this city. The Naxi worship the sources of water as the places where gods of nature live. Pollution of water is absolutely forbidden, as well as to cut down trees around the source of water, or even to cry loudly (Yang 1999: 48, 56, 66).

Naxi buildings in Dongba pictographs, from left to right: Tent, the primitive home of the Naxi when they were still nomads, shelter, straw hut, wooden house, stockade village, stone stockade village, walls, city, temple, pagoda and palace.

The hidden symbolism of Naxi houses

The building of a house supposes a permanent rupture of the natural environment. Therefore, it must be accompanied by ceremonies aimed to restore the equilibrium and to prevent the Shu nature spirits from leaving their place, as the grounds are disturbed by excavating for the foundations, the digging up of rocks for the building, the cutting of trees, etc. (Rock 1952: 13).

Naxi houses consist of two, three or four buildings, erected in a rectangular configuration with a courtyard in the center. Houses, reflecting the cosmic and social forces that order the Naxi world, are arranged following the dualist idea that configures their worldview as expressed in the two buildings essential to all Naxi homes. The main residential building contains the kitchen, larder, living area and sleeping

136

quarters; it is the focus for the social life of the family and the place for entertaining guests. Directly opposite is the stable, which provides shelter for some combination of horses, mules, sheep, goats and cattle. The opposition of the house to be stable within the family compound replicates the external distinction between village and wilderness, agriculture and pastoralism (McKhann 1989: 163-164).

It is possible to find a number of diverse dwelling forms among the Naxi, with the villages between Yongning and Lijiang illustrating the gradual transformation of Naxi society along history. Thus, while the Yongning type may be considered the original style, found in the Naxi territory before the beginning of Chinese influences, and the courtyard compounds presently found in Lijiang the acceptance of the Han Chinese building methods, the Naxi population between Yongning and Lijiang show a gradation of Chinese influences, perfectly visible in the dwellings styles (Li Pingping 2005: 9, 24).

"All houses in Lijiang had two storeys and were built with three or four wings. The lower part was of sunbaked bricks, whitewashed on the outside or coloured in orange, yellow or even light blue, according to the owner's fancy, with elegant borders traced in black or blue. In the centre there was a stone-flagged courtyard with three stone-lined raised flowerbeds. The lower rooms in the middle of each wing had four or six doors all beautifully carved in filigree. Other rooms had either carved or latticed windows. The back of the rooms was wainscoted in wood to conceal the ugly bricks. The upper storey was one vast room, sometimes quite low, and it could be partitioned into as many small rooms as one wished. Since few

Naxi liked to stay upstairs, it was usually used as storage for provisions, crops and goods. There was no ceiling and as the wooden walls never quite reached the roof, breezes circulated freely. It had a few windows in the outer wall and a continuous series of windows facing the courtyard which could be opened by tilting them upwards. The roof consisted of heavy clay tiles, with the corners slightly curved upwards in the usual Chinese style. All tiles were of gray colour, but sometimes the monotony was broken by white lines along the border" (Goullart 1957: 34). Naxi traditional houses have a wooden superstructure and rough plank roofs weighted down with stones. They combine in terms of arrangement, structure and appearance some characteristics of buildings found in China during the Tang and Song dynasties with components and architectural styles that reveal the influence of the neighboring Bai and Tibetan people. During the Qing dynasty, the Naxi absorbed alien architectural techniques and combined them with their traditional knowledge, forming a unique ethnic feature known as "three rooms plus one screen wall," very popular in the Lijiang old city and "one courtyard plus five skylights," characterized by rooms surrounding courtyards, wide corridors, and auxiliary corner rooms. The appearance is simple but lively with finely crafted elegant fixtures. Buildings, screen walls, floors, doors and windows, as well as paintings and carvings on beams reflect clearly local characteristics. Houses are often fronted by water channels and backed by river lanes. Sections of some houses span over water and others diver waters into their courtyards (Zhu, Shi and Sun 1998). The arch over a gateway is an important part of a traditional house. The suspended fish on the gable of the house is both an architectural decoration and a magic defense for suppression of fire and lighting. It also symbolizes the people's desire for surplus every year (the Chinese character meaning fish is pronounced like other meaning surplus) (Yang 1999: 56).

In Baidi Township, traditional courtyards are wooden houses often composed of several parts: The main building, a herbage building, a corral, a small "flower room" and an entrance surrounding a rectangular yard, sometimes without a fixed layout. The main building is always orientated south, divided into 3 or 4 rooms; it is able to accommodate almost all the daily life activities of every family member. The threshold is high while the lintel is low to protect from cold and wild animals. The roof is set with wooden sheet with a hole that serves as both as a chimney and to adjust the temperature and light indoors.

At the gate of each traditional house there are two protective stones that symbolize the god Lv and the goddess Se. They are not only the creators and civilizers but also the first human ancestors, the first couple, the ancestral couple, the brother and sister that intermarried to propagate the human race. They are considered the yang and the yin, the two poles that started the movements of the world that led to creation. They were instrumental in the survival of the human race, as they warned Congrenlien about the upcoming flooding and the ways to avoid it, and introduced him a suitable wife to re-create the world. Sometimes there is a drawing of a yak and a tiger on paper, considered also protecting deities of the gates, because when Lv and Se went down to earth, Lv rode a tiger and Se a yak. Both animals have the power to distinguish gods from demons and good from evil. After the marriage of Lv and Se, the two stones on the gate are a continuous reminder that the marriage between a man and a woman is the most suitable. The white color of the stones, as a symbol of the transformations of the souls after death, is believed to have the power to provide long life to the people living in the house (Mu 2005).

Inside the house we find again the dual worldview of the Naxi. In the center near the hearth there is a father post and a mother post (Mu 2005: 392). The main post in the house is the Heaven's prop (Muan dtv). It rests on a central father pillar indicating Heaven's as well as man's power erected in the middle of the house. It is the *axis mundi* of the house, as it represents the Junaruoluo Mt., the center of the world. It supports the central roof beam (regarded as female), as well as the free corner of the hearth. On it are hung three twigs, one

Traditional Naxi house with the Heaven prop at left. Lijiang Museum of Dongba Culture

from each tree in the Worship Heaven ceremony, which underscore the essential continuity that exists between the values expressed in this ceremony and those reflected in the structure of the house (McKhann 1989: 157, 168). To its left side stands the mother post with animal bones hanging on it, as offerings to the Non gods of the domestic animals. On the corner there is a bed, and a tablet of ancestors above it, where the people will pray on each meal, and in front of it a kitchen (He Shangli 2000). The space defined by the central post and the two walls on the south and east is the social center of the house: A raised platform made of earth bricks with a triangular hearth in the center, and seating and sleeping areas along three of the four sides, where the family eats its meals, entertains friends and relatives, and spends the evening hours in conversation (McKhann: 1992). Each of its four sides has its own symbolic associations, which together form an ordered set. By the south wall is the area used exclusively for men's activities, called the "big bed," because is where the male household head makes his bed facing the ancestors. The area by the east wall is for women's activities. It has the wife's bed, called the "small bed." Women are forbidden to enter any of the exclusively men's areas. In the corner between them stands a bureau known as the god shrine, on which offerings of food, wine and incense are placed at every meal and in conjunction with major ritual occasions, such as weddings and funerals (McKhann 1989: 164-5). On the roof usually there is a small hole, where a pine branch symbolizing the god of victory is inserted.

This sacred fireplace constitutes the cosmic center of traditional Naxi homes. The hearth consists of three cooking stones that represent the God of the Hearth; three is a sacred number and these stones may perhaps stand symbolically for the three stones used in the Worship Heaven ceremony (Jackson 1979: 95). The symbolism of the three stones in the hearth is common to many peoples living in southwest China. Whenever anyone drinks tea or eats food, he will first pour a little of the tea or food on the three stones, a libation to the spirits of the ancestors and to the Sv life god. North of the hearth (or sometimes in the kitchen) is a shrine for the Sv and Non spirits which protect the family and beasts respectively; inside it reside the 18 Non spirits that protect the animals represented with 18 stones in a circle. In it are placed also 18 pine cones representing sheep; a flail, grass, a miniature trough with salt, a rake and a bamboo stick (Rock 1972: 347).

The Sv life god is not an ancestor but a protective spirit that guards a person's soul. Every person has a life god; all life gods of one family live inside the sacred basket which hangs above the hearth, from where they protect the members of the household. The Sv are propitiated daily by pouring libations on the three hearth stones: *ssu* also means three. When a death occurs it is believed that the deceased's Sv life god flies over the hearth and the dead person is called *Sv-Mun* (Jackson 1979: 244). Inside the basket there are some objects offered to the Sv gods full of symbolic meanings: a pagoda, a ladder, an arrow, a yellow oak sacred stick, a sacred stone, five color silk strings or cloth stripes that represent the five main elements of life, namely wood, fire, earth, metal and water, and a bridge. A sacred pagoda made from green cypress represents the place where Sv rests; the pine ladder represents the necessary path that the god must pass to bless the family with luck and

142

prosperity. The connexion of human beings with Heaven through the Sv god is suggested in a pictograph that shows a couple ascending the ladder to the realm of the celestial god Zilao Apu. "It is here inferred that all husbands have ascended the ladder of the spirit of Life to the realm of Zilao Apu to obtain the nine rocks and nine loaves of butter of Ho, the spirit of the male semen and having received them, are descending again to earth" (Rock 1962: 94). The ladder is also a reference to the shamanic character of Naxi culture, as shamans use a ladder to ascend to the sky, and gods and dead souls are said to descend to earth by means of ladders (Stutley 2002: 31). The arrow of the Sv life god has three barbs and is used in the marriage ceremony. The three arrow head segments represent three generations in a family: Grandfather, father and son (He and He 1999: 39; Rock 1972: 510). During the weeding the groom holds in his left hand a wooden pagoda and a claw, while the bride holds in her right hand two objects representing a ladder and bridge. "By means of the ladder and bridge (tools for crossing gaps in vertical and horizontal space), the bride is said to arrive at the groom's house (pagoda), whence she is prevented from leaving by the holding power of the claw. At the end of the ceremony, the presiding Dongba binds the four items together with red string and places them in the house god basket" (McKhann 1989: 171). The sacred stones symbolize the wish for an unending longevity for the lineage, as they are considered as stable as the sacred Junaruoluo Mountain (Duncan 2011). After Worship Heaven the tree branches are carried home and are put in the Sv basket, as a symbol of the continuous prayer for good luck to these gods (Mu 2005: 43).

Naxi traditional Dress

In the past the Naxi had no other material than hemp, which they wove in narrow strips of about a foot wide that were sewn together (Rock 1962 116). They don't dressed too many clothes, and even on snow sometimes they walked barefoot. "When the weather is very cold they wear a sheepskin. During the imperial era, the chiefs dressed as the Chinese, but their wives did according to tradition. All of them, irrespective of their age or gender, liked to carry a knife as an ornament" (Bacot 1913: 120).

In the folklore of the minorities of southwest China there are some myths that establish a relationship between the traditional dress of the women and the first steps of male dominance in the society. Sometimes it is the belt, or the apron, anyway women's dress is linked with the loss of their power and of their sexual freedom. As the different kinds of ethnic clothes indicate the proper attire that women must wear along their life cycle and their marital life, it became a public reminder of what can be or cannot be done according to local custom. Naxi feminist activists have already noted the cultural meaning of the ethnic traditional dress and the influence of Chinese culture on its changes, which divided Naxi culture along patriarchal gender lines by advocating Chinese-style dress for Naxi men and not for women. Current representations of minority dress manifest themselves as predominantly women costumes. As a consequence, the younger generations of minority women reject their traditional clothes in favor of Western dress in order to fit in with dominant Han culture. The only young women in Lijiang who wear Naxi dress put on this clothing when they work as tour guides, at cultural events and on special occasions. When the older generations of Naxi women die out, so will do Naxi traditional clothing.

Naxi traditional dress can be divided into three styles: Lijiang and surrounding plains, the Baidi area, and Eya isolated communities. In Lijiang Naxi women wear wide-sleeved loose gowns accompanied by jackets and long trousers, tied with

Lijiang city from the Lion Hill

richly decorated belts at the waist. The most distinctive component is the sheepskin cape, usually made of one whole piece of sheepskin (maybe related to the Qiang people worship of sheep), black on top, and white on the bottom, symbolizing earth and heaven respectively, with fleece to the inside. The cape is tied across the back with two long cotton straps. The cloth extends a little at each shoulder, to resemble the body of a frog, one of the totemic animals of the Naxi, venerated in ancient times as a harbinger of rain, which in this way extends

145

to Naxi women its protection and its generative powers (Goodman 1997: 52; Mu 2005: 343).The cape is not only for adornment, but to protect their bodies, as Naxi women bear a heavy burden of physical labor all their lives, such as farm work, trading and housework, and most things which have to be transported are carried on human shoulders (Zhang 2001: 130). On the shawl there are two large embroidery discs, one over each shoulder, representing the sun and the moon, and seven round patterns symbolizing seven stars. That tells why people say that Naxi women "carry the moon and the stars on shoulders" to imply they work diligently from before dawn until dark (Yang 1999: 75). Some myths tell that the first woman who wore it was the heroine Yinggu, which after put an end to the pains inflicted by the eight suns that scorched the earth, put seven of them on her sunshade wrap, leaving only the moon up in heaven (Zhang and Zeng 1993).

In Baidi Naxi women wear a long tunic blouse, a long hundred-pleat skirt, a colorful woolen sash round the waist, a pair of black boots in cloud cluster style, a white furry goat skin cloak on the back, and wind braids around their head. They also wear a sheep skin coat similar to the Lijiang one. The girls are dressed in black and white skirt, with a white goatskin on their shoulders. They wrap their heads with colourful silk threads; some may even wrap ten silver plates. Married women are also dressed with black coat and white skirt, but their goatskin is black and their heads are decorated simply with colourful bands. Senior women dress the same clothes but they wrap their heads with a black handkerchief, and wear a black skin on their shoulders. As for men, they are all dressed white

146

with a red band around their waist, wear a hat and black boots (He Shangli 2000).

When the Naxi move to a new home they must burn all the old clothes they don't want to carry with them, because they think that souls inhabit different parts of the body, even in the shadow and the clothes of a person, and if their enemies get their clothes they get their soul, and can therefore harm them. Souls can move freely out of the body, especially while dreaming. They can leave the body from different places but they must enter it again through the place they left. Then it is very important not to move the body of a sleeping person.

As the main regional trade center during centuries, the Naxi developed around Lijiang a flourishing industry of handicrafts and wares, being the most famous their manufactures of leather, especially in Shuhe, which included all the elements needed by the tea and horse caravans, as well as cooper ware. Bronze locks, containers, and decorative products were some of the most appreciated Naxi products, usually traded as far as south Yunnan and even Calcutta in India. More surprising was for modern researchers their paper-making techniques, still alive in some of their traditional communities, developed and preserved by the Dongba priests who need paper to write or paint their books, their sacred paintings, divination cards and other religious paraphernalia. While the Mu and aristocratic families used paper made following Chinese techniques, Dongba priest kept their traditions, maybe for religious reasons, transmitting with their knowledge a primitive and simple way of paper making. They slowly wash, pound and boil fine strips of the bark of the *Wikatroemia mekongensis*, which is later spread, separated and dried. With this process

147

they obtain a strong paper on which surface is easy to write and draw.

Women's financial clubs

A special characteristic of their social life are the women clubs (*tso* in their language) that through their seasonal meetings and their activities of self-help, contribute to enhance the social cohesion of the Naxi women. Their original function was to provide means of financial support among the different families of a community, as in most of the families women still manage the financial needs of its members, providing money not only for everyday activities but also for weddings, funerals and other special occasions, as well as natural disasters or calamities. According to their legends these organizations of mutual help were devised by their celestial ancestral mother Cunhongbaobai, as a way of allowing women face unexpected events successfully. Different formulas consecrated in the customary law allowed women borrow money from the coffers of the club, with the compromise to give it back, without interests, as soon as possible. Sometimes the social cohesion of these lender groups is strengthened by periodical banquets shared by all the members, in which every woman will pay a small amount of money, creating a common fund ready to help those who need it (Guo 1998: 241). In some areas these societies have developed beyond their original aim and holding beneficial activities regularly, contribute to enhance the social cohesion and financial solidarity within the whole village, becoming the nucleus of the local organization of villagers.

Among the Naxi staple food the most characteristic are the ubiquitous *baba*, a kind of flat bread made of wheat, filled with a sweet or salty content that can be eaten for breakfast, lunch or dinner. Easy to carry and to be eaten anywhere it is at the same time tender and delicious. Much more elaborate and difficult to carry is the pea jelly sold everywhere in the Naxi villages. In the past many families brewed their own Yinjiu wine, a sweet and fragrant wine made of highland barley and wheat and sealed for long time.

CHAPTER 5

Naxi
Life Cycle

The changes in the situation of the Sv life god present
in every human being constitute the stellar moments of the life
cycle of the Naxi. The proper care to the Sv god along the main
stages of human existence is the best guarantee of a happy life
for the person, as well as for his or her lineage as a whole. We
see along the rituals that mark the life of the Naxi, a continuous
effort to ensure that the Sv life god follows his proper course,
with ceremonies that stress the moment it enters the child after
birth, other paying respect to it, as being present in the Sv
basket of the family, blending the Sv gods of the spouses during
marriage, and merging it again with the big soul of nature after
death. As the Naxi consider that the return of the Sv life god to
the realm of nature is specially dangerous in a time when this
spirit is more powerful, and his influence on the living people
can be more harmful, rites designed to avoid this danger are so
prominent that some authors think that "death is the rite of
passage par excellence", with different funeral ceremonies
depending upon the social status of the deceased, and special
rites for those who have died unnatural deaths (Jackson 1976:
85).

Birth

The rituals performed at birth suggest that in the Naxi traditional thought the entering of the Sv life god in a person is a gradual process developed during the last term of pregnancy and the first days of life, and that this process is considered complete in a first phase, when the new born is one month old[14]. Before this time, lacking the protection of the Sv life god, mother and child, considered especially vulnerable, are carefully protected and object of some taboos, with the mother usually fed with chicken soup and eggs, not being allowed to bathe or wash her hair, nor to go out of her courtyard (Pinso 2006: 150). In Baidi, where the traditions are better preserved, when a woman gets pregnant she avoids those tasks requiring more physical effort. As she is considered unclean, she must observe different taboos. In the time of delivery she is assisted by the two future grandmothers who would take the newborn once he is born, cut the umbilical cord with scissors, and wrap his belly with a cotton cloth. The placenta is wrapped in vegetal paper and put in a jug, then buried near a tree or in a not much trodden place, with the umbilical end facing up, lest the baby

---

[14] Among the many ideas regarding the human soul some Naxi scholars think that the fetus has one soul, children that can walk and talk have two souls, children have three, youngsters have five, women with sons have seven and men with children have nine. Other Naxi explain that there are three main souls: one residing in the heart, one in the neck and one in the back, frequently massaged after drinking or eating. These three souls would correspond with life, speech and thought (Bai 2001).

151

will suffer from nightmares. If during this process some problems appear, the members of the family will pray to the gods and ancestors to protect mother and child. Three small stones are hung on the main door of the house to let the people know that a child has been born, as nobody can visit this home at night. In some villages the same day of birth a Dongba is called to perform the ritual of getting rid of the dirtiness. To do it, he will carve a horse with wood of black willow and a puppet with eyes, mouth, and nose with a branch of red willow, as well as some magical implements to expel the evil spirits. He will put all these things in a basket near the heaven prop, and will read some chants to purify the house. The climax of the ceremony is when the Dongba, after sprinkling water on every member of the family, sprinkle some water on the body of a chicken, which is immediately sacrificed, symbolizing that it will take away all the impurities of the family (Yang 2008). It is interesting to remark the presence of the horse both in the first moments of life and in the last ones, and to remember its role as a spiritual carrier in shamanistic religions. In villages around the Lijiang plain the third day after birth a Dongba is invited to worship the God Sanduo with a chicken or a pig for giving a name to the newborn.

The first month of life is a time of important spiritual adjustments, as shown in the tradition that prescribes that until the newborn reaches one month, the members of the family would burn incense and pray the gods and ancestors every day. When he is one month old, the mother would wash her hair and would invite a Dongba to celebrate a simple ceremony of *Guide the child to go out*, when the Dongba sings his prayers opening the road and the mother follows him with the child at her back. A ceremony with an interesting parallelism with this other performed after death, when the Dongba would open the road again, this time to the ancestors' realm. The child must have a needle inserted in his cap and a little sickle hanging from his neck, to avoid the attack of evil spirits. After opening the road they can go back home, where friends and relatives would present the new-born with *baba*, rice and pork, and the Dongba would choose a name that must be related in a magical way to the age and horoscope of his mother (He Shaoying 2001: 166-170). The fact that the baby isn't called by his name until he is one month old shows that the Naxi think he is not a person until this age, possibly because this is the time the Sv god needs to enter his body.

Children are usually breastfed until they reach one year old, when their milk is officially stopped, though sometimes it goes on for some months. To stop the baby from drinking milk they have some methods, as separating mother and child during one week, smearing the mother breasts with pork bile, or drawing dreadful designs on the mother's breast. Then the child is fed three times every day with corn porridge. During the first year of life the babies are not washed (He Shaoying 2001: 166-170).

Rites of Passage

The rite of passage among the Naxi marks the moment when the child, having nurtured during his infancy years the seed of the Sv life god, completes this process. Having got the generative powers that would correspond to their gender, Naxi youths are welcomed to the adult life. Though some authors think that there is no rite of passage among the Naxi, there is no doubt that in the past these rituals were performed in all Naxi territories; nowadays they have been preserved in some places, consisting mainly in ceremonies of changing clothes. It seems that before reaching age the Sv life god is not completely developed inside a person; the main aim of the ritual being to provide to the young the correspondent share of the Sv life god to become full members of the family. This moment is symbolized by a chicken tied to the incumbent. Naxi people consider that a man is adult at 13 years old because he has already lived and passed through a cycle of the 12 elements, and his Sv god is present in the family Sv basket as part of the family soul residing in this basket, that links all of them with their totemic ancestors. After death his soul can be send to the ancestors' lands (Mu 2005: 38-9, 161).

Dongba pictographs show the role of the women in Naxi society, from left to right: To mate, man and woman under the Naxi yin-yang, yak and tiger; to consult, talk over; big, the vagina of a woman; ancestral home, a woman inside the house; a big tree, mother, a big woman.

In Sanyuan village, when the child reaches 13 years of age, a Dongba will be invited to chant to the Sv god, praying him to provide the youngster with good luck and fortune. This ceremony is related to the supposed ability of the new adult to carry on a productive life and bring new lives to the family. The first aspect seems to be guaranteed by the fact that in some places this ceremony is performed in the granary; the second by the need that the person that helps him or her to put adult clothes, must belong to a healthy family with many sons and daughters; the whole ceremony seems a ritual confirmation that the Sv life god is ready to inhabit an adult's body. In Baidi this ceremony usually coincides with the New Year, and is celebrated when the children reach their ninth or tenth year. These rituals are similar to those of the Yongning Moso, where the "dressing the skirt" ceremony marks the adulthood of girls, the moment when they will be allocated a *flower room* inside the house, where they would sleep and would receive their lovers at will. Dressing the skirt ceremony is therefore the starting point of the sexual freedom for the Moso women, a freedom of which Lijiang women were excluded due to the influences of Chinese culture. Its sexual connotations can help understand the reason of the almost complete disappearance of this ritual. If we suppose that in the past Naxi women enjoyed the same sexual freedom than their Moso sisters, what is very likely due to their cultural, geographical and linguistic relations, a simple way to end with this freedom would be to abolish the ritual that started it.

Men and Women

Before talking about love, marriage and sexual relations, it will be worth reading the interesting description of the situation and activities of women in 1940s Lijiang provided by Peter Goullart. Women were traditionally considered unclean creatures that may not sit in the presence of men or eat together with them. As it was not right for them to walk above men's heads women never slept in the upper rooms or remained there long. As in the rest of China, laws did little to protect women. Wives could be bought and sold, and widows could be disposed of by the eldest son. "Continuous manual work was the women's lot. They did not revolt; they did not even protest. Instead, silently and persistently like the roots of growing trees, they slowly evolved themselves into a powerful race until they utterly enslaved their men. They learned all the intricacies of commerce and became merchants, land and exchange brokers, shopkeepers and traders. They encouraged their men to loaf, lounge and to look after the babies. It is they who reaped the golden harvest of their enterprise, and their husbands and sons had to beg them for money, even if only a few pennies to buy cigarettes. It was the women who started courting men and they held them fast by the power of their money. It was the girls who gave their lovers presents of clothes and cigarettes and paid for their drinks and meals. Nothing could be obtained or bought in Lijiang without women's intervention and assistance. Men knew nothing about the stocks in their own shops or of the price at which their goods should be sold. To rent a house or buy land one had to go to those women brokers who knew about it." The owners would not negotiate without the women brokers' expert advice. Tibetan caravans, on arrival, surrendered their merchandise to the women for disposal; otherwise they ran a risk of heavy losses (Goullart 1957: 137).

Because of their manifold activities and the heavy loads of merchandise they transported on their backs from house to shop or from one market to another, Lijiang women had developed superior physical characteristics. They became tall

156

and husky, with great bosoms and strong arms. "They were self-assured, assertive and bold. They were the brains of the family and the only foundation of prosperity in the household. To marry a Naxi woman was to acquire a life insurance, and the ability to be idle for the rest of one's days... and as the Naxi men outnumbered women by five to four, a man was lucky to find a wife at all... She was his wife and mother and, moreover, she kept him in clover. What more could a man want? There was not a single woman or girl in Lijiang who was idle. They were all in business from early morning till night. No family could possibly have a female servant. It was utterly unthinkable. Why should a woman slave for somebody at a few dollars a month when every day of her time was worth so much more? The wives and daughters of the Naxi magistrates and other high officials, of the wealthy merchants and landowners, worked as hard as any humble village woman. Either they specialized in selling the Tibetans' merchandise at the local market or went down to weekly markets in Heqing, carrying the goods in baskets on their backs. Or, perhaps, they heard that some villages had cheaper potatoes or pigs, and off they would go, bringing the loads back and making a tidy little profit. Many a time I met Madame Hsi, the magistrate's wife, carrying on her back a heavy basket of potatoes or a sack of grain" (Goullart 1957: 138).

The open admiration that Goullart felt for the Naxi women did not preclude him of having also a high opinion about the men: "In extolling the physical strength and business acumen of Naxi women I do not wish to imply that Naxi men were effeminate or cowardly. Since the earliest days of their history they have been renowned for their bravery, courage and loyalty. It certainly needed pluck and resource to come down all the way from Tibet and defeat the aboriginal tribes which dwelt at the time in the Lijiang plain. The contingents of Naxi soldiers have always been the mainstay of the Yunnan Provincial Army, and when called upon they fought to the death. It was through the participation of the Naxi troops that the famous Taierzhuang[15] victory over the Japanese was won. They never turned their back on the enemy and very few survivors were left. They are intrepid horsemen, tireless walkers, and can exist for months on a meagre and monotonous diet" (1957: 142).

Love and Marriage among the Naxi

An analysis of the kinship terms in Naxi language and the older myths preserved among them suggest that in remote times Naxi ancestors enjoyed free love and marriage in a society that was possibly matriarchal. During the initial period of patriarchal society women still could marry more than once, enjoying a high degree of sexual freedom. Naxi myths show that before the first post-flood ancestor Congrenlien married the goddess Cunhongbaobai, and started the practice of the pairing marriage, the ancestors of the Naxi enjoyed sexual freedom in a way maybe similar to the Axia visiting marriage of the Moso. Chinese influence on the Naxi started in the 14th century with the adoption of the basic values of Chinese's culture by the Mu Kings, and grew slowly until 1723, when the

---

[15] This battle, in 1938, was one of the few victories of the Chinese army over the Japanese in the Sino-Japanese War, and maybe the most famous.

beginning of the direct implementation of Chinese laws and regulations put an end to the freedom of Naxi women, establishing monogamous patriarchal marriages in which the maternal uncles, as a vestige of the old matriarchal society, had the privilege to choose daughter-in-laws among their nieces. The marriage was arranged by the parents from the time of their children's birth, with the help of fortune-tellers and matchmakers. When the spouses were thirteen or fourteen years old, it took place the small marriage. After it, they started to know their new families and visit one another frequently, until marrying definitively six or seven years later. It is possible that their old family structure resembled that nowadays still alive among the Moso of Yongning, where free love and matrilineal families are widespread, with the girls living in the *room of flowers* after puberty, where they can receive their lovers at will. Independently of the length of their relation, the men always leave the women's room in the morning and return to their mother's family, without any right to the children product of this relation, which will belong to the mother's family.

Some Dongba manuscripts point out to a time when the Naxi lived under matriarchal clan organization and women enjoyed a higher position. As the pictograph for the "fence" that enclosed matriarchal clans, the ancestral home is depicted as a woman inside a house, pointing that it was the mother's home. Usually the concept of big is associated with women and that of small with men. "To pair" is in Naxi woman-man, "a couple" is called wife-husband. Chinese historical chronicles inform that women can interpose between men's fighting and stop them (He Zhiwu 1989: 82, 102-5).

The establishment of Chinese gender relations into a society so different brought serious problems to the Naxi. While the young Chinese lived most of their youth in a society characterized by gender segregation, finding few chances of meeting people from the opposite sex, and so, of falling in love, the Naxi enjoyed freedom to meet and love people from the other sex. This freedom, and the banning of keeping sexual relations to unmarried people, in the age when the romantic

Love process among the Naxi, as seen in Dongba pictographs, from left to right: Companionship between man (at left), and woman (right, with headdress), they like each other, they dance together, love surges among them (it seems that the man has a flag or a flower in his hand); they get married (before a Dongba), and live as husband and wife (with fire on a three stones' hearth). Below, a couple at home, the wife gets pregnant, she gives birth to a baby, and she carries the baby in her arms. Some problems can happen. The last two pictograms are for infertility, vaginal discharges are seem, and divorce.

feelings are most common and the sexual desire most urging, brought unending sufferings to the young Naxi. If a deep feeling grew between a boy and a girl, it was difficult to reach a happy end, because usually the parents had already arranged their marriage when they were very young. Pregnant girls were forced to abort; and their descendants, excluded from the family and society. As young people had no say in their own marriage, elopement and suicide were common among lovers who could not live together legitimately (Zhang 2000).

Chinese cultural influences, on the other side, expanded from Lijiang in a centrifugal movement, in a way that waves of influence could be identified, slowly weakened as they went further from Lijiang on to the mountainous regions. Diverse geographical and social conditions, as well as the contact with different peoples, provoked that the Naxi maintained a variety of familiar structures and marriages. Among the Naxi living in isolated districts sexual mores and marriage traditions are much freer, being possible to find a gradation of sexual and marriage freedom between the matrilineal society of the Moso in Yongning and the rigid sexuality of Lijiang city. If we examine the three main routes that communicate Yongning and Lijiang, we would find that all the three are inhabited by populations (ethnically Naxi or related with them) whose sexual behavior is in the middle of those characterized by Yongning and Lijiang. "In La-pao, a district several stages north of Lijiang within the Yangtze loop, where Naxi still live a very primitive life, it is no disgrace for a woman to have children before married. When a woman marries for the first time her children follow her to her husband's home. In other districts, girls given in marriage remain with their husband for one or two months, and return to their parents' home. They can only begin to live with their

161

husbands if they give birth to one or two children, remaining otherwise in their parent's home" (Rock 1939: 1). In the northwest route Li Pingping discovered that the structure of the Naxi houses in Baidi reflects a transition from the matriarchal structure of the Yongning houses and those of Lijiang, with some *rooms of flowers* to receive the daughter's lovers, still used among them. He Baolin (2004: 175) found in Baidi and Eya marriage customs that could be considered halfway between those of Yongning and Lijiang. In the isolated communities of Baidi still remain houses where the youngster move after adulthood, where they meet their partners of the opposite sex, and spend the night together. After the wedding the bride returns to her parents' home, and sometimes she did not start to live with her husband until her children are four-five years old: -children who could be the fruit of her sexual contacts with other men. In Eya there is the marriage of some brothers with the same wife, as well as women who choose not to marry but to remain with freedom to choose their lovers (called friends) at will. In the northeast route, the Taluo[16]usually marry inside their race and enjoy great sexual freedom, with men and women living with different partners along their lives, and the young girls leaving their parents' houses to live with other girls of the same age in a "girls' house", where they receive their lovers at will. They can enjoy short-time relations before reaching 25 years old more or less, when they usually make a simple wedding with the person they

---

[16] Taluo people, officially considered belonging to the Yi nationality, live near Yongsheng. Among them young girls are encouraged to have sexual relations, and the marriage link is very weak, with frequent divorces.

love. Divorce is simple also, as it is to remarry again (Ceinos 2011: 95).

In the Naxi ideology of gender relations, marriage is thought as a relationship between bone and flesh. Naxi speak of a person's "bone" and "flesh" kin as those persons related to him/her through men and women, respectively. Sons are bone, daughters are flesh. The father is bone, and the mother is flesh. The opposition between bone and flesh also reflects the predominance of male authority in society. Men are like mountains, fixed in one place; women like trees that move around and attach themselves to the mountain (McKhann 1992).

The original sense of the wedding is the separation of the Sv life god from the wife family Sv basket and its establishment in the husband's family Sv basket, wedding being a fusion of the Sv life gods of husband and wife (Mu 2005:42-43). In Naxi language wedding is called "To receive the Sv god" for the name of its main ceremony, when the Sv life god of the bride, is carried from her parents' home to that of the groom. A complex ceremony in which special care must be taken not to carry with the life god of the bride the Sv god of any other member of the family, neither the domestic gods that provide fertility. The ceremony begins in the bride's house, where the go-between (called white crane) and the Dongba (called *xusun*) go the day before the wedding. There they will take out of the Sv basket the ritual objects usually inside it: the pagoda, ladder, bridge, arrow and stone, and would wash them, putting some grains inside the basket. In the bride's home courtyard a pole will be erected from a pine branch. The day of the wedding the bride will wash her hands for the last time in her father's house, symbolizing that she will not cause further problems to her parents, and will cry expressing her grief for leaving their home. While the family of the groom takes some of the pine branches from the pine pole, expressing that they are carrying away the bride's fertility power, the Dongba must take care to avoid that no other domestic deity follows her Sv god; to do this, he will put a little butter in the head of each of the members of the family while praying: "The Ni and Nuo of your family cannot leave; the god of cereals, the god of the domestic animals cannot leave; the god of birth cannot follow her and leave." Sometimes these gods are also blocked with a white cloth (Yang 2008: 13).

In the groom's house a new basket is arranged. When the bride arrives, a woman who has children must wash her hair, while a man shaves the groom's hair. Then the Shu nature god is worshipped in the courtyard, and a sheep is sacrificed. After it a ritual which includes putting butter on the foreheads of the new couple is held to put the Sv life god of the bride into the Sv basket where the life god of the bridegroom's family resides. The holding of this ritual indicates that the bride formally becomes a member of the bridegroom's family, and that their marriage is completed. The essential aspect of this ritual is to join the souls of the bride and groom together, and allow the soul of the bride to become part of the life god of the groom's family and never depart (Duncan 2011). The pine branches carried from the bride's house are put in the groom's courtyard while a prayer is read to Congrenlien with the hope that the fertility granted to his marriage by the gods would be provided also to this new couple. The groom and his bride are entwined with a cord that is considered the thread of the gods;

this cord has been previously tied to the Sv or life god, and it is supposed to assure long life. The Sv is offered food, a lamp, butter, incense, wine, etc. All the Shu nature spirits of the region are invited and beseeched to grant fertility (*nnu* and *o*) to the bride and the groom (Rock 1963: 436; Yang 2008).

Only after this ceremony is performed, the Naxi consider that two persons are married. It's the same if they perform a "marriage by kidnap" or they fly away together. Until the moment when the Sv god of the bride is separated from her family Sv basket and carried to her husbands' family, they are not considered married. From this moment her Sv god is in her husband's house, and if one day she returns to live in her parents' home, she cannot share the first meal of the year, where all the family souls are together, not give birth in this house. At death her funeral must be performed in her husband's house, where her Sv god resides, and if is not performed she may be transformed in a roving spirit (Mu 2005: 138-160).

Death and Funerals

If death is the crucial moment in the life of a person, among the Naxi is especially important for being the time for the final transformation of their Sv life god, and the beginning of a series of changes that will make the Sv god must leave the Sv basket and transformed in ancestor travel to the ancestors' land. To avoid that the Sv god common to the family follows the dead spirit, the Dongba must perform a ceremony that brings the family Sv back home (Mu 2005: 39, 44). The main aim of Naxi funerals is to provide the dead with all what he may need to reach the land of the ancestors, being the ability to reach the ancestor's land what will decide whether his soul become a god or a demon. Heroes and chiefs are gods; wicked people are demons because after death nobody would provide them with their needs for the road. If the descendant is cut off, a man can not travel after death to the ancestors' land and becomes instead a roving demon that blocks the road to other dead souls and the generative powers of people. Chinese and Tibetan influences are shown in the concept of a way full of obstacles that the dead must pass through, the paradise as an arrival place and the belief in a rebirth (Mu 2005: 66-67, 154). Therefore a set of ceremonies were developed with the aim of ensuring that, whatever situation the dead had to confront, there would be a proper way to allow their soul to enjoy a happy journey to the land of the ancestors, and not to remain as a headless demon disturbing the living or causing illnesses and disasters.

When a person dies his soul can be transformed into three different entities. If he experiences a proper death, and the proper rituals for release the souls from purgatory are performed, the soul will be led to the ancestors' realm where he will become an ancestor. If the death is also considered correct but there is no chance to perform the release of the soul rituals, the soul cannot reach the ancestors' realm, and will become a hungry roving spirit, usually fed with offerings not destined to him. If the person experiences an abnormal death his soul will become a demon, which can cause sickness and misfortune to the living ones (He Baolin 2004:20). When a person dies the relatives are afraid that the soul remains near the body, and acting as a ghost, causes misfortune to the people. To avoid this, they cremate the body and force the soul to leave it and travel to the ancestors' lands. Souls are symbolically associated with shadows, which are afraid of light. This explains the presence of the sun and moon in Dongba ritual clothes, and the taboo that forbids to cut the hair or the nails at night, for fear that the shadow will linger in them (He Baolin 2004: 18). The belief that the soul of a person, at death, can be transformed into an ancestor, protecting and granting fertility and riches to his descendants, or into a demon, causing illnesses or misfortunes, already explained above, had great influence on the funerary rituals of the Naxi. Of the several ceremonies performed in the three years that follow death, the most important are the Zhima ceremony performed the day of the funeral and the Khinv ceremony, that three years later, ends it with a big banquet.

When a person has breathed his or her last, the relatives place some grains of rice "and a silver coin under his or her tongue, an act aimed at provide food for the journey and silver to pay the spirits that could block the road" (Zhang Xu 1998: 127). It was believed that if the grains were not placed, the soul would be taken by the seven female wind demons who control the wind, and not reaching the realm of the ancestors they would become roving spirits, which as the constant companions of the wind demons, can cause hail-storms, illness, etc. (Rock 1939: 5)[17]. Therefore, when a person is ill, weak or very old, there is always one member of the family watching by

---

[17] This concept would be familiar to westerners, as among the old Greeks a coin was placed in the mouth of the dead to pay Charon to allow the crossing of the Stynx River. Similar traditions have been reported in Central Asia and India (Miyamoto).

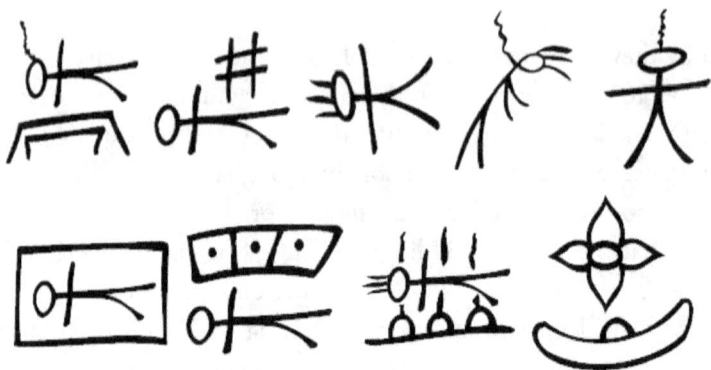

The death process in Dongba pictographs, from left to right: A person sleeping, on a bed, his breath ascends to heaven; a person sick, the bed is near him; a person dead, with three hairs from the head symbolize that he is now a demon, a person hanged, the rope could be seen; longevity, a dead person inside the coffin, buried, and burned. The last pictogram stands for soul, spirit.

the bedside day and night, and it is considered a calamity to die suddenly in an accident or a fight (Goullart 1957: 63-4).

It is the belief that man has five souls, the protecting deity, his double or shadow, his demon-soul, the dtu embodiment of the evil principle, and his own soul inhabiting his body. These five souls are the result of the belief that when a person is born, he came forth from the five elements; when he dies, he is broken up into the five elements; and when he is cremated his body is again dispersed into the five elements (Rock 1937: 118).

Once death is confirmed a Dongba is sent for, but as nobody from a home in which a death has occurred is allowed to enter another house until after the funeral, the priest is called by throwing a stone against the gate of his compound. In this way, he will know the reason for the bidding and will take two books with him, one to determine the particulars for a rebirth of the departed soul and one to chant magic formulae. When the Dongba arrives he will examine the corpse to find out from which orifice the soul has escaped the body (Zhang Xu 1998). The corpse is then sat up in bed, a lamp is lighted and placed in one hand (left for a man, right for a woman) while the Dongba tells to which deities the lamp has been lit. After the body is washed and dressed in a burial robe it is laid in the coffin and covered with a large piece of cloth like a sheet. The coffin lid is closed and four plates of food and one bowl of rice, with one chopstick laying across it and one chopstick sticking straight up out of the rice, are set nearby. The family doesn't cry or mourn until all this is done.

On the funeral day, a white couplet is hung on the doorway of the courtyard where the deceased lived. White cloth is wrapped around the head of the mourners for the next few days. A blue or white couplet is put up on the first anniversary of the death; a yellow one marks the second anniversary. The day after a funeral, relatives visit the graveside to offer food and drink and to kowtow in front of the grave. Then, seven, fourteen, and twenty-one days later, relatives return to the home of the deceased to pay their respects and share a meal. The same thing happens for the first and second anniversaries of the death. At the third anniversary the end of the mourning period is celebrated by hosting family members and friends to a feast, and the white aprons worn during mourning time are changed and a red couplet is hung in the gate (Pinso 2006: 133-142).

In Baidi, when somebody dies, people will shoot into the sky to notify friends and relatives. Then they wash the corpse and put him into the coffin for people to show their

Tortures in the Road to Heaven. Yunnan Provincial Museum

condolences. On the eve of sending out the coffin friends and relatives of the dead will say goodbye to him singing dirges all night long. Next day a Road to Heaven is set to send the dead

170

to the world of gods. Finally they send the body to the furnace to cremate the body, and they collect the ashes in a bag to be preserved in a cave (He Shangli 2000). Cremation was substituted by burial in Lijiang due to Chinese influence after 1723. Elaborated funerals were held for anyone with three generations of living descendants, as his death is considered an event worth celebrating, and for the chiefs, when horses were presented and ritually accepted by the heir, then they were suffocated and the other presents ritually broken to be sent with his spirit (Jackson 1979: 128). As the ancestors arrived on horse the soul must also ride a horse to their realm. Every person road to birth is also on horse. Because horses were used at chiefly funerals, it was told how animals died and the origin of the horse was chanted (Jackson 1979: 130). A sheep or a cow is led in and offered alive to the deceased; it is then taken out and killed. A sheep is offered with the aim that the illness of which the person has died, that is believed remains with the corpse, be transferred to it through a purification ceremony (Rock 1937: 88-90). Sheep and horses are considered natural psychopomps. That is, guides in the road that the soul must travel after death. There are some myths relating the origin of the sheep as a soul carrier. Traditions regarding the horse are spread all around western China, from the Mongols living in the Northwest to the Burma border. Horses are not only considered ideal carriers of the death soul, especially of the chiefs, but in any spiritual travel the soul performs, as the shamanic travels the shaman does to contact the spiritual beings causing illnesses to a person or bringing bad luck into a community. The use of the horse for the last spiritual journey of the chiefs may indicate that in the past, most of the chiefs were also shamans; and maybe they were chiefs because they were shamans. The Naxi have many types of funerary ceremonies, with a lot of books belonging to them. The largest one is performed for a deceased Dongba. For deceased laymen there is the Zhima funeral, actually the opening of the road for the soul to the land of his ancestors, when the deceased is set on the path to the ancestors and told not to return, and the body is taken to the cremation ground. Long strips of white cloth used at funerals of people who have died far from their home represent the path which the soul is to follow from the regions where the body died. This white cloth acts as a bridge to the souls. The *Hazhipi* (Road to Heaven scroll) also acts as a bridge for the soul to reach the realm of the gods (Rock 1937: 40 - 41). This is a kind of long scroll painting used for funeral and "releasing the souls of the departed" rituals. In the morning, the scroll is unrolled and attached to the head of the coffin, and the Dongba chants the words of the scripture entitled *Guiding the souls of the departed on the Road to Heaven.* The long painting is a road guide that describes an arduous journey on which the souls of the departed have to be tortured in hell, with the possible sins the living soul could have committed and the punishment that they are causing in the afterlife graphically described. After the soul experiences the pains of this purgatory, is reincarnated as a man again. The Road to Heaven reflects Naxi social morals and concepts of life, as they believe that a person's evil actions in this world would, usually related to the lack of respect to nature or to human society, produce the *lenchou* demons in the next. These demons block the way that the souls of the departed have to travel. Only with the help of the Dongba the soul can pass the blockage of the *lenchou*

172

demons. Every man is punished in a different way according to the sins he has done in his life. Some souls of the deceased are stopped in Hell for they were steeped in iniquity during their lifetime; some meet troubles but they still could walk into "Man's world" with the help of the Dongba, and reincarnate as human ancestors; a few kind people could pass all of outposts easily and get to the heaven and become deities, finally joining the world of the gods and the thirty-three-storeys of Heaven (He and He 1999: 60; Li Xi 2001; Jackson 1979: 134-7). Punishments shown in this section are almost identical to those that can be found in Buddhist temples and Tibetan mandalas or Wheels of Life (Yang 2000: 60).

When a big Dongba dies, the ritual of Worshiping Dongba Shiluo must be held in order to guide his soul to the founder's side in the 18-storied heaven one step after another along the sacred road painting (He and He 1999: 34). During the course of the ceremony the altar, scroll painting and offerings table are arranged in the house of the dead. The ploughshare represents the sacred Junaruoluo Mountain. The offerings, such as dough figurines of white yak and horse, bamboo weaving, tea drink, etc., are hanged there. The Road to Heaven scroll is laid from the bier of the house, through the courtyard to the gate, meaning that with the help of the Dongba, the soul of the dead will walk along the sacred road to Heaven (Li Xi and A Yuan 1998: 38).

Sometimes a wood carving representing the dead Dongba, dressed in his clothes and carrying his sacred implements, is put on a paper horse, and with the help of an assistant is slowly carried along the stages of the sacred road that the officiant Dongbas are reading. Among the Rerke

173

people living in Baidi, the sacred road can be symbolically represented in the courtyard of the deceased, with the carved image of the dead is slowly carried along it, riding a horse or a goat (Yang 2000:52).

The Naxi believe that after death a person is changed first into a snake, and only becomes an ancestor after the Khinv ceremony has been performed. Thanks to the fire funeral the snake can take out her skin and became an ancestor. The place of incineration is called "place where the snake changes skin". After sending the soul of the departed to the ancestor's lands, every year they are invited three times, on the 3rd, 6th and 10th lunar months (Mu 2005: 182-4). Khinv ceremony must be performed within three years of the death of a person, lest his or her spirit cannot be escorted to the realm of the ancestors. A whole community must perform it together, with one family presiding and others furnishing a sheep as offering to the dead. During the ceremony about one hundred manuscripts are chanted. The body of the deceased is represented as a pine branch into which eyes, mouth, etc., have been carved. At the end of the ceremony all the *nv* (pine branches) are wrapped in a piece of cloth, and the son of the deceased who presides at the ceremony mounts a horse, but facing back. He rides thus with his back to the horse's head, carrying the *nv* to a cave near the village. Afterwards a ceremony to send the *nv* effigy by a rope bridge, across the river separating the living from the dead, must be performed (Rock 1972: 473, 780). When somebody die before the ceremony of adulthood, they must wait for the death of an adult of the same family to carry his wood image to the cave, which means that the soul is going to the ancestor's land in the company of the adult's soul, because his soul cannot go alone. The wood image of the people that die without descendants cannot be carried to the cave, because his soul is not going to the ancestor's land, as they are afraid the lack of offspring could be transmitted to other families (Mu 2005: 190).

In some places, after the corpse is burnt in the cremation place, they bury a small piece of coal, and every year on the 5th of the sixth lunar month they make sacrifices to the place where the coal was buried, asking the spirit to come back to visit his family. After three years there are no more sacrifices (Bacot 1913: 122). As any deceased for whom the Khinv ceremony has not been performed is considered a demon, the Ts'u nv or funeral for a demon must be performed. "To redeem the soul from the hole in the ground" is a small ceremony performed when a body is transferred from a grave to another considered more auspicious, when the soul is requested not to remain in the old grave but to follow the body to the new one (Rock 1972: 472). Special ceremonies are performed when a person dies a violent death, like a soldier on the battlefield and for whom *Harlalluku* has not been performed, because it is thought that they can return to their family and provoke illness.

During the funeral there are two simultaneous services rendered to the dead soul, first is to show the way to the ancestor's land. A way remembered in all detail, which after 80, 90 or more than 100 stops, will render the soul in the realm of the final destination. This land of the ancestors is considered a geographical territory, the place from where the ancestors started their migrations, and surprisingly, each of the Naxi branches send their deceased's souls to a different place. Myth and history blended to point out the land of the ancestors, because many of the sacred roads end in Junaruoluo Mountain, the place where the first post-flood ancestors Congrenlien and Cunhongbaobai arrived in this world, when they descended from Heaven. Junaruoluo is the place where heaven and earth communicate. All souls are therefore, led to the threshold of heaven. Only the Dongbas' souls are led into heaven (Yang 2000). The second is the Road to Heaven, where the obstacles that the soul will find in its way are meticulously described, as well as the way the soul will surmount them with the help of a Dongba, which chants the sacred scriptures and dances frenetically expelling the evil spirits that block the way of the soul with his sword. It seems that the concepts of a hell, purgatory and heaven have been superimposed on older traditions that stressed only the need to carry the dead to the ancestors' lands. In Junaruoluo live the Shu spirits of nature, and in this way we find one more relation between the Shu spirits of nature and Sv life gods, which came from Junaruoluo, spend most of the person's life hanged near the symbol of Junaruoluo and at death return to this mountain, the realm of the Shu (Yang 2000).

There are some myths that point out that in the past the body of the dead mother was ritually eaten to transmit her abilities to her sons and daughters, as they believed that if they do not eat her body they will be changed into monkeys and when they eat it again they will be changed into human beings. In other myths the gate deities Lv and Se instruct human beings to divide among them a tiger skin, as the tiger was considered the deity that provided the human beings all their abilities, and transmitted for the first time knowledge and power to the human beings. By means of the tiger skin they get its wisdom and power. Any food the Naxi eat is not only considered a way of satiate hunger but also a kind of total strengthening related to the appropriation of the spirit of the animal or plant ingested. Eat the mother was seen as a way of keeping her power within their descendants. The tiger was created from many elements of nature, and human beings learned from the tiger as the myth *The Transmission of wisdom* narrates. The wisdom of the parents is transmitted to their sons and daughters at death, in the form of their own bodies or through the skin of the tiger. And when there is no tiger skin, the Dongba has a way of feigning it, painting the lines, etc. The transmission of power from parents to children can be done also through clothes, as the presence of the soul of the dead is thought to linger in the clothes and objects he left, which cannot be given to any person not belonging to the family[18] (Mu 177-180).

The Naxi believe that after death one soul remains in the body. This is the soul that can transmit the power of the living person to his descendants when they eat his corpse or when they remain in the place where he lived. To make

---

[18] This concept must not surprise the reader. Other minorities, such as the Zhuang, have similar concepts (Ceinos 2011). Han Chinese also believed that the power of the dead person is transmitted to those who eat his flesh. Missionary's narrations describe that in the 19th century, people in Yunnan fought to eat the flesh of a famous bandit, in the hope to acquire his bravery (Dennys 1870). Christians also ritually eat the flesh of Christ. Among the Hani when an old man dies, his eldest son succeeds his breath. Literally his son inhales his last breath like artificial respiration, as if after finishing his life of this world, the soul of a man continued to live in his lineage eternally (Miyamoto).

effective this transmission of power a special ceremony is performed, in which the parent's powers are symbolized by a tiger skin, which he forward to his descendants. The power of the soul is also transmitted from mother to son after the delivery.

When one of the human souls leaves the body, the person becomes ill. This is because the Shu spirits of nature seduce or catch the human souls. Therefore the healing ceremony would consist in searching the soul and making the Shu free the soul. But if the soul does not come back and the sick person dies, after death the ceremony to call the soul must be performed. The mother can also call the lost soul from the gate of the house[19].

Land of Suicides

Lijiang is a suicide land of the world. Every family may find one or two members who committed suicide for love. To die for love is not viewed as a humiliating matter but as an easy and sometimes ideal way to escape from the complexity of love affairs, such as losing face, fierce quarrel, fatal shame, unhappy marriage, etc. (Goullart 1957). Before the communist reforms of 1956 there was a high index of suicides among the Naxi, most of them committed by young people who, rather than separate from the loved one, to marry the partner chosen by the parents, preferred to commit suicide. When the lovers decided to commit suicide, they dressed their better clothes, and left the village, sometimes to hang up themselves together in the same

---

[19] These kinds of ceremonies were in the past very common among the Chinese and other indigenous peoples of Yunnan.

tree, losing their life with the hope of being happy in the paradise. These practices were highly ritualized, as were the four methods of inducing death: hanging, drowning, jumping off a cliff or swallowing poison (black aconite or opium) (Hsu: 1998). The marriage system of the Chinese, designed for a society spatially segregated along gender lines, was difficult to adapt to an environment where boys and girls interacted freely during the age when romantic feelings and passionate love are due to arise. The way to solve this contradiction between Chinese rules and Naxi mores was the suicide of the lovers. In Lijiang the migratory pressure of Chinese's males and the response of the Naxi to keep their lands and culture, avoided the implementation of some valves of escape, as the "marriages by kidnap" that among the Naxi living in other areas, allowed the most romantic youth, to fulfill their dreams of love. Suicide can be related to the imposition of Chinese's mores, as in the places where the young enjoyed freedom to choose their couple, as in Baidi, suicides were not frequent.

Suicide was not a sudden decision, but was carefully considered and arranged, as the ritual required buying new clothes and ornaments with the aim of appearing elegantly dressed before the gods. It was postponed until the day when the results of their intercourse become apparent, or if not such intercourse has taken place, to the time when one of the lovers was to be married to the party selected for him or her. Lovers would select an inaccessible or lonely spot on the Jade Dragon Mountain, allowing a beautiful view over the surrounding country, where they would build a shelter, sing and play the mouth harp, eat specially prepared food, and live as a married couple before committing the ultimate act of romantic protest.

On the selected day they will live their love to the full until the fatal moment, and then hang them on a convenient tree. Sometimes as many as six couples will go together to die in the forest (Rock 1939: 2).

It was believed that the souls of suicides ascended to a heaven of their own: The Third Kingdom of the Jade Dragon Mountain, where they will enjoy free love without getting old, without pain nor suffering, flies nor mosquitoes. Where people will ride tigers and deer, that sometimes plough the fields, and clouds will make their dresses. Only the souls of people who die for love were supposed to be able to enter this kingdom. A kingdom ruled by the goddess Youzu and the god Guodu, whom ride a red tiger and a white deer, play the flute and the Jew's harp, amid flying birds and happy beasts. There the lovers will remain young forever, and will never separate. A paradise that seems a return to nature, to the life before social constraints transformed it, where people could not only enjoy the free love forbidden by their society, but to live in harmony with the animals of nature, in contrast with a working life in which man uses and destroys nature (Yang 1999).

As these beliefs were put forward by the Dongbas, some writers blamed them for the epidemic of suicides by lovers. The fact is that to listen to the description of this kingdom during the chanting of the myth *Lubanlushao* in the *Harlalluku* ceremony induced many youngsters to end their lives in the mountain to reach this paradise. Some Dongbas tried to avoid it beating strongly their drums to difficult the understanding of its description, or chanted it in the deep night. Admonitions in the first chants of the *Harlalluku* ceremony for the part of the parents about the need to enjoy a

180

long and prosperous life were supposed also to discourage lovers to put an end to their lives. During the *Harlalluku* a carved image of the dead, dressed with a cloth, was hung on a rope symbolizing it was crossing the river. After the crossing the rope was cut.

Suicide was not only a way out of life for romantic lovers; men and women, alone or in small groups of friends, are known to have committed suicide also. The reason for the frequent suicides among the Naxi must be searched not only in the imposition of the Chinese marriage system, but also in their concept of the soul and its transformations after death. It seems that besides the traditional belief that a person who dies without the grains put in his mouth would become a headless roving wind spirit, there must have been other concepts that would not consider suicide, as the warrior death far from his family and parents, as a gate of an afterlife full of potential threats to the dead family. Narratives of suicides' and warriors' paradises sometimes characterized in ideal terms must have provided alternate ways to the afterlife, which made both suicides and warriors deaths, consistently fit with the Naxi worldview. The lost of importance of Naxi warriors, when the Mu kings lost the political and military prominence in the area in the 18th century, and the dramatic increase in the rate of suicides, as a result of the enforcement of Chinese sexual conventions, must have led to an effort to hide the concept of afterlife paradises and consecrate the sedentary way of dying as the only suitable for a person.

It seems that at the beginning there was no concept of karmic retribution, just the difference between souls that are feed by their descendants, becoming gods, and souls that are

not, becoming demons. The origin of the Third Kingdom of Yulong could be related to the need to find an acceptable place for the souls of the warriors who died out of home once the Naxi have their military ethos well established, or even to encourage these warriors. This ideal kingdom must have caused some suicides, but not everybody believed in it, and not all suicides were entitled to enter it. People were supposed to secure the entrance to the Jade Dragon kingdom carrying a stone, on which their names were written, becoming registered residents of this ideal kingdom; a kingdom that can be related also with the old land of the ancestors, or with the first concept of Junaruoluo Mountain, indicating that the young suicide was to be happy forever. In all funeral rituals, whether the dead soul is carried to the ancestors' land (normal death) or to the Yulong Kingdom (abnormal death), the aim of the ritual is to carry the soul back to the realm of nature, from where it emerged to inhabit a living body (Yang 2000).

A relationship could be established between patriarchal power, settled way of die, travel to the ancestors' realm in one side and free love, matriarchal society, outside life and death and travel to paradise on the other. Having in mind what we already know about Naxi religion and culture, it can be suggested that the outside paradisiacal death would correspond with the matriarchal time of the Naxi society, when mother earth received in her boson all her sons. The presence of queens and female demons as well of the fact that in their old tradition, the thread of the life was in the hands of the goddess Yulludumi, who spun the white wool thread of longevity (Rock 1972: 493) are facts that point in the same direction. Orthodox ways of thinking about the proper way of death would reflect the patriarchal stage of society, with the filial piety of his sons being a necessary step in every person's road to become an ancestor.

CHAPTER 6

Naxi

Yearly Cycle

The yearly cycle of the Naxi consists of a series of ceremonies performed to renovate their right to inhabit their present land, with rituals aimed at obtain the blessings of territorial spirits and to keep the ancestors in a distant honorable position; they mark also the main steps of the agricultural cycle. These ceremonies reflect their border character, as they show deep influence of peoples living around them, being celebrated sometimes in the same dates and with a similar content. Indigenous local traditions, regional and imperial influences were assimilated by the Naxi to mark every year with the moments when it was supposed that the communication with gods and ancestors was open, making them witness to the renovation process involved in the New Year, as well as guarantors that the adjustment with local spirits that would provide enough food to live one more year, would be successful. Ancestors, territorial deities and the chance of a bountiful harvest, are all related in a society that every year suffered hunger during some of the spring months, when food stocks were low, and a delay of the rain season could mean the death to some of its members.

Chinese influences are specially manifest in the celebration of the New Year, the cosmic adjustment of time presided by the emperor in Beijing, that all peoples under the orbit of the Chinese empire must dutifully follow; a foreign tradition that slowly displaced in Lijiang the indigenous New Year, around the 8th of the second lunar month. Many indigenous peoples of Yunnan celebrate their main festival this same day as the Prince Festival among the Bai living in Shaxi, the Sun Festival among the Axi Yi of Mile, the Sword-ladder Climbing Festival of the Lisu, the Sheba Festival of the Kucong, the Flower Festival of the Yi in Chuxiong, as well as one of the main Buddhist festivals. It is possible that before the beginning of Chinese influences this can have been the time when most of the populations of Yunnan province celebrated the New Year, and renovated their pact with sacred nature that allowed them to enjoy its fruits one more year.

Worship of Shu Nature Gods

There are strong arguments that support the idea that in the past the main ritual activity performed on a temporal basis was the worship of Shu nature spirits on the first days (usually on a dragon or snake day) of the second lunar month, and that this was the traditional New Year of the Naxi. In Baidi, where the old traditions have been preserved, this is the most important festival, when everybody dressed in their best clothes, gathers around the Baishuitai terrace in a festive atmosphere and pay respect to the Shu gods of nature. The first day the Dongba arranges the ceremonial ground, with trees and branches that represent the nature spirits and ceremonial paintings of gods and demons. When the offerings are ready the Dongba narrates the origin of the Shu nature spirits and their relationship to the human beings, asking the Shu to provide good winds and rain, and a good harvest for the coming year. Two hens are offered to the nature spirits, as well as the head of a pig, killed without any special ritual, whose meat will be shared among the families present. The second day each family will go to Baishuitai to worship the Shu nature spirits. In this day the Dongba play no special role, but sacrifices and ceremonies are performed by the head of the family. On arriving each family would pay homage to the sacred spirit of Baishuitai touching the white rock with their heads. Then a hen would be offered to the Shu in the Dragon Pool, its blood scattered around the altar, while its feathers, salt and pine branches, continuously burned, seem to guarantee that the message reach the gods through the smoke. Some roasted grains of rice or wheat, called flower grains, are thrown as an offering to the Dragon Pool, with the idea that the gods of nature will give them back a good harvest. Each family has a fixed place at the feet of the mountain where they worship the gods of nature in the New Year and Torch Festival. Each of these places has a small altar, usually three stones leaning on a tree trunk, and some benches for the family to seat. Families are reunited around their sacred spaces, where they will make some offerings in their altars to the spirits of nature. After the ritual lunch is finished, they will sing and dance together. Before leave the place the people, traditionally the main woman of each family, take holy water from the Dragon Pool; which will be used to make the food that will be offered to ancestors and deities. Some people even wash their face and hands with the holy water, or soak a tree branch in the water to take it home.

Worship of Shu Nature gods is the most important of all rituals which take place at the village level. It is called "repayment of debt to Shu" stressing the idea that along the year the people invaded many times the realm of the Shu, and therefore they have a debt to pay. The ceremony is an enactment of the agreement reached in mythical times between men and nature with the help of Dongba Shiluo, and a call to the need to preserve this harmony. During it, the people pray the Shu to forgive all their transgressions and to provide good luck. This ceremony is especially important when there has been a long drought. When people or their domestic animals are sick, a minor ceremony would be performed (Li Jingshen 1991). The character of this festival is clearly related with other agricultural ceremonies that marked the New Year and the renovation of the world. After the main ceremony in Baishuitai, Naxi people living in more isolated villages would worship Shu in their own sacred mountains. On these days every person adds one year to his or her age and rites of passage are performed, when boys and girls celebrate the ceremony of "dressing the trousers" or "dressing the skirt" in a full granary symbolizing the hope to have enough food and clothes to wear in the future (Outlook 1999: 206).

In this same day it was celebrated also the Herders' Day, when the masters let the young herders a free day and give them good food and some gifts, and they gathered in the mountain to celebrate a banquet and enjoy their festival (Guo 1998).

Sanduo Festival

Around the same time when the Shu Nature spirits are worshipped in Baidi, the people gather to honour Sanduo in Baisha and Lijiang. Being Sanduo, the god of the mighty Jade Dragon Mountain, under whom protection both Lijiang and Baisha were established, the most powerful of these territorial spirits of nature, and the most important of the mountain gods. He is also a hero, good at warfare and always ready to help the poor and troubled. The main protector deity of the Naxi, depicted wearing a white armor and riding a white horse. In his cult we find that the territorial deity of the Mu clan became a national deity when they reached national preeminence[20]. It explains also the exclusivity that the Mu kings enjoyed in the worship of Sanduo, as "it was the custom for the ruling chief of the Naxi to come to the Beiyue Temple on the 8th day of the second moon to worship Sanduo. In olden days, when they were the native prefects of Lijiang, and they came to the temple to worship, none of the peasants were allowed to remain in the neighborhood, still less in the temple. It is believed that Sanduo was born in the sheep year, and so on a sheep day of the second moon the Naxi peasants flock to the temple by the thousands. Much wine is drunk and many brawls ensue, as gambling takes place on that day" (Rock 1947: 197). Nowadays Naxi people gather before the statue of Sanduo in Beiyue Temple or in

---

[20] This phenomenon is very common not only in China and East Asia but also among the ancient Greeks and other distant peoples.

188

Lijiang's Black Dragon Pool, kowtow to his statue and leave offerings to him. Later, every family holds another ceremony at his private residence (Zhang and He 2005: 106).

The performance of these rituals just before the start of the agricultural activities suggests that both are part of the same concept: The worship the territorial and nature gods to secure to the people the fruits of the land, as the Naxi must appease the local deities to reconfirm their rights to occupy lands that in the past belonged to other people.

Worship of Heaven ceremony, celebrated some days before Worshiping Shu, is a ritual celebration to remember that Naxi ancestors came from Heaven, and that therefore they descend also from a celestial lineage. Both brotherhood with sacred nature and descend from celestial ancestors celebrated in these two main festivals, emphasize the sacredness inside every person, a sacredness that will be ritually cared for in a short ceremony celebrated between these two: The worship of Sv life god, which is performed to avoid that the life gods of men, animals, or grains leave the house. To do this, they take out the sacred elements contained in the Sv basket, wash them and put them inside again, as well as some grains. Then tea and wine are offered to the Sv gods and a prayer is chanted: "We see off the old year and the old month, we receive the New Year and the new month. We offer sacrifices to the Sv above asking for the year to be good and auspicious, asking longevity and peace. We ask the Sv god for protection, to not call the souls of the family members to travel idle to the land of the demons. Please protect us, do not call the god of the animals neither the god of the grains." Then a goat is killed and its blade shoulder is offered to the god (Yang 2008: 23).

The second month was traditionally considered the month of the gods, because it was believed that the gods descended to the world and roamed among the people. In this month they worshipped also the water gods, the Mountain gods, and the village gods. The first day of the second month a ceremony to pray for sons or daughters is performed beside the Heaven prop by the couples that having being married for some time, have not yet children. To this aim they use a wood plank in which the Ren spirits with the shape of butterflies, as well as the sun, the moon, stars and the sacred mountain Junaruoluo are drawn. The Dongba chants a short manuscript to the deity in charge of the birth, and the sacred objects that usually hang from the Heaven's prop are washed and put again in their place (Yang 2008: 65).

Worship of Heaven ceremony (Muan bpo)

The religion of the Naxi is the cult of Heaven, a supreme being doted of infinite attributes (Bacot 1913: 15). Of all ceremonies performed by them Worshiping Heaven is the oldest and the most important. Li Jing, a historian of the Yuan Dynasty, wrote: "The Naxi climb up the mountains on the fifth day of the first lunar month to worship the heaven." Joseph Rock thinks that this ceremony "dates back to the days when the Naxi were still nomads, living in the grasslands of northeastern Tibet, where they led a primitive life with their herds of sheep and yak" (1948: 7). Naxi people call themselves the nationality of worshiping heaven because it is the performance of this ritual to worship their ancestors and the forces of nature what distinguishes them from other ethnic groups. The Naxi are quite conscious of this, and so every performance serves to re-establish ethnic boundaries. This ritual keeps interesting common points with similar ceremonies performed during the Chinese Zhou dynasty: "The way and the contents of the Worship of Heaven ceremony of the old Naxi and that of the old Zhou are the same, both used three beasts to sacrifice, big incense, white chrysanthemum and offer butter, grains and wine, both are celebrated in the suburbs. The lay out of the sacrificial objects and the arrangement of the sacrificial space, all is the same" (Chen Lie 1988: 9). Some of the old songs chanted during the performance of the Naxi worship of Heaven shown strikingly similitude with old songs found in the Chinese Book of Poems, and the Nine Songs of the Chu Elegies (Chen Lie: 2000). This suggests that Worship of Heaven was one of the features of Naxi old culture, originated even before they were a differentiated ethnic entity. The old Qiang are historically and culturally related with the Zhou Dynasty. Many historians consider that both they are branches of the same trunk, whose culture diverged when one of them, the Zhou, settled in the fertile valleys of north China, while the other, the Qiang, remained as nomad herders.

The Worship of Heaven also bears many resemblances with rituals for worshiping the ancestors among neighboring groups like the Qiang and the Yi. Christine Mathieu considers that this ceremony was modeled on the *she* rites of the Chinese, which not only established "the Naxi race as the people of the Mu chief, and the Mu chief as a representative of the emperor. It also placed the Mu's realm inside the Empire." She believes that it "reflects the economic and political modes of sedentary, agricultural people who came under Chinese influence" being

191

its prayers for descendants, long life and grain "at the change of the seasons in tune with Chinese agricultural calendar" (Mathieu 2003: 292-295).

The origin of this festival is mythically related to the first ancestor, Congrenlien, which after his arrival on earth realized that without the blessing of his parents-in-law, he and his spouse would remain childless. Thus, a go between was sent back to Heaven to find out by which measures the favour of the parents-in-law could be gained. He returned with a precise description of Worship of Heaven Ceremony (Oppitz 1998: 176).

The Worship of Heaven belongs to a general class of Naxi periodic rituals to obtain *neeq* and *oq*, the male and female elements of reproduction, which are distinguished from funerary and demon-eviction rituals by a relative absence of Buddhism symbolism. In ancient times the Worship of Heaven must have been a simple affair, performed by the head of the family without the aid of a Dongba, which even today are seldom invited to perform the ceremony (McKhann 1995: 56).

This ancestral rite was performed by the male members of patrilateral kin several times a year. The main one taking places on the first moon. Outside every Naxi village there is one place to Worship Heaven for every lineage living in it, as each of the four Naxi lineages (Mai, He, Shu, Ye) worship Heaven separately, usually situated near some old trees, or surrounded by a large grove of trees especially planted with a small wall of earth and a stone gate, and in the center another stone for sacrifices (Rock 1948: 12). The altar is crowned by three trees. A juniper flanked by two oaks: The Chinese Emperor between Heaven and Earth. On the other hand, according to the myth

192

relating the marriage of the first earthly man, the juniper is the heavenly uncle, and the oaks are the celestial father and mother (Hsu: 1998). Big incense sticks, offerings and sacrifice are arranged at the feet of the sacred trees. After a confession of sins before the ancestors, they will chant the scripture named *The descend of Man*, to memorize the ancestors, praise the heroes of creation, transmit their historical origins, strengthen unity, and pray for favorable weather and peace (Li and A 1998: 18). In Baidi during this ceremony no people of other families is admitted, nor could they speak other language than Naxi, even some words and expressions are exclusively used in the ceremony. A ceremony that was slowly transformed from a sacrifice to heaven to a sacrifice to the ancestors, and now ancestors worshipping is its main content, with the old men telling the lineage history, and the young holding competitions of riding and shooting (He Shangli 2000: 58- 29). Archery is one of the most important activities, useful in old times to remark the fighting will of the lineage; the Naxi main allegiance being with the lineage, nor with the ethnic group or the village (He Zhiwu 1987:10).

Some days later the five oldest men who celebrated the worship of heaven, got together again to worship the god protector of the village, represented as a red band hung from a pine. These five men are a vestige of the time when the elder's council ruled every village. Worship of Heaven must be studied together with other rituals of worshiping nature forces, including those celebrated to worship wind, water, stars, mountains, trees and stones. All elements of nature are believed to have the power to influence the life and welfare of human beings, whose fate is thought to be linked to the stars. The stars

193

are prayed to provide long life in ceremonies when 28 branches are set around an altar (for the 28 celestial sites), and the seven wind goddesses are asked to provide good harvest (Bai 2001).

The four seasons in Dongba writing, from left to right: spring or the windy season (three gust of wind under the canopy of heaven), summer or the rainy season (three drops of water falling from heaven), autumn or the harvest season (with a plant growing on the earth), and winter or the snowing season, with three snowflakes falling from heaven.

It is interesting to remark the ritual complementarity of the three main festivals of the Naxi, with Worship of Shu Nature Spirits performed at the village level, as a pact between a community and the nature they use, the Worship of Heaven, celebrated at the lineage level, is related to ancestors, while the New Year, with its national characteristics, only gradually imposed among them the concept of belonging to the Chinese empire. These three ceremonies also reflect three different historical stages of the Naxi. Being the Worship of Heaven the most primitive, dealing only with the basic cult of the ancestors and the need to keep the continuity of the lineage, maybe in a time when they were still nomads, or struggling to find a place in a territory inhabited by other peoples. Worship of Shu nature spirits reflects a posterior time, when the use of the natural resources of a fixed territory had become the norm, and the Dongbas had already established themselves as mediators between men and nature. It adjusts the people to this territory. The New Year, as a national ceremony common to all the peoples inside the Chinese sphere of power, marks the political adjustment of Naxi in this realm. Lineage, village, nation, three politico-social entities originated in three different historical periods are celebrated at the beginning of the year, the intensity with which each of them is celebrated among the Naxi living in different places reflecting the relative importance of lineage, village and nation among them.

On the other side, the content of the Worship to Heaven and the Worship of Shu is similar, both of them are prayed to ask for good rain and winds, fertility and health for persons and animals. They symbolize Naxi cult of the ancestors and of nature. Worship of Heaven is a worship of ancestor's ritual with some elements of a nature cult included. Myths chanted in both ceremonies could symbolize the moment when the leader of the Naxi nomad herders, Congrenlien, is received by the daughter of the local tribal headman, Cunhongbaobai. Other Naxi myths that stress the nomad character of Congrenlien and the agricultural knowledge of Cunhongbaobai also point out that this foundational myth of the Naxi could tell the history of the transformation of their forefathers, from their nomadic way of life to one of settled agriculturalists (He Limin 1985).

Worship of Heaven is also a ritual to the pairing marriage in which the husband married in her wife's family. Originally both men and women performed the worship of heaven, as shown in witnesses' writings from the Ming dynasty.

195

The origin of the worship of heaven could be the worship of ancestors, as we see that the two oaks symbolize heaven and earth, (father and mother), and the juniper in the center is the lord, the emperor. The maternal uncle, the main protector of the family under the matrilineal family becomes the emperor under the Mu family influence. In worship of heaven the celestial ancestors are worshipped, all of them on the feminine side, the father, mother and maternal uncle of Cunhongbaobai. The central role of the uncle points out to matriarchal times, when the uncle was the main protector of the family. This is the reason it was later substituted by the emperor. Worship of Heaven is a reminder of the celestial connection of the Naxi ancestors, and their idea of the presence of the divine within every person. There are some similitude between the ancestors' worship of the Moso and the worship of heaven of the Naxi. When the Mu got to power, they transformed the worship of ancestors in worship of their heavenly ancestors, and then of heaven, and the maternal uncle was transformed in the emperor, new guarantor of the protection to the Naxi people. The Naxi, as the people who worship heaven, are the people that worship the celestial ancestors of the Mu kings and their own ancestors (Mu 2005 105-114).

New Year

The New Year is nowadays the main festival for the Naxi of Lijiang. In the Chinese realm the establishment of the calendar was a ritual task of paramount importance, a prerogative of the emperor, with any issuing of alternate calendars being considered heresy and treason and therefore

196

severely punished[21]. The integration of the Mu kings into the Chinese empire must have been followed by their acceptance of the imperial calendar; with their traditional festivals celebrated in the wake of the New Year celebrations.

As in the rest of China, the New Year is considered a time of renovation for humans, their houses and their fields, a time of spiritual and physical rebirth when every person must be born again, clean and uncontaminated from the hard existence of the previous year. Cleaning the houses and courtyards from top to bottom signifies sending out the bad with the old year and bringing in the good with the New Year. Foot washing the last day of the year has the same meaning. The physical and spiritual cleanness could be related to the visit of their ancestors and their will to appear before them in their best outfit, as well as to their efforts to expel the evil spirits, as if the physical removing of the dirty and the old would carry with it spiritual effects. To keep at bay evil spirits they hang red colour New Year couplets (two long strips of paper, one pasted on each side of the doorway, in which auspicious desires are written in a poetic style) because spirits are afraid of the red. A shorter, four-character saying is pasted across the top of the doorway. They also light firecrackers outside their front gate before sitting down to a meal, to frighten away spirits and to

---

[21] "To issue a counterfeit or rival edition was a capital offence. It was an infringement of the Son of Heaven's authority to regulate the empire. The making of calendars, and the sciences of mathematics and astronomy on which it was based, were part of imperial state power, and therefore closely guarded. The issuing of calendars was by the same token part of the unification of the empire conceived cosmologically as 'all under heaven', the making of calendars was part of the task and the power of cosmic adjustment" (Feuthwang 2001).

celebrate the fact that everyone is considered one year older on New Year's Day (Pinso 2006: 32- 39).

During the last days of the year, people are busy shopping for the festival. On New Year's Eve they would roast a pig head and kill a chicken, as chicken's soup and pig's head are standard items on New Year's Eve menu. Another traditional dish is *ch'er*, a slice of local bacon; a part of a very fat boneless, fleshless pig (Pinso 2006). To make the *ch'er* a pig is cleaned and opened in the middle lengthwise. All the bones and meat are removed, and only the fat is left adhering to the skin. It is then heavily salted and spices are added and then it is sewn up again. They are left, pressed and flat, for several years. On festivals slices of this meat are cut off, dropped in boiling water for a few seconds and then eaten (Rock 1963: 39).

On New Year's Day the young men would offer wine and sweets to their elderly relatives, and the whole family would go to pray before the tombs of their ancestors, who are believed to have returned home to spend the New Year with the family. As burial grounds are usually located in the mountains, people make a short trip there, women carrying baskets with food and woks, and men with hoes and axes for clearing brush from the graves. After all the graves have been cleaned, a male representative of each family in the clan lights incense sticks in front of every headstone. They then sprinkle alcohol and tea, place some food, wine and cigarettes in front of each tomb, and kowtow before each graveside (Pinso 2006: 41- 44). Besides worshipping the ancestors, other religious ceremonies must be performed in the New Year, including the worship of the God of the Hearth in an improvised altar, and worshiping mountain gods, a remainder of the time when the

198

Naxi forefathers were nomad herders and hunters and depended of the mountain for their livelihood (He Pingzhen 2003). On the first day and the fifteenth of the first month, villagers would burn incense near a pond, a spring, or a pagoda as well as on the sacrificial altar at home.

At night all members of the family must be reunited, with chopsticks and tableware put also for the absent ones. First they feed their dogs, because according to their myths the dog gave human beings cereals, and they observe carefully how the dog eats, because they believe it can forecast if the grain and meat would we plenty in the coming year. After the second day they will feast other friends and relatives, as Naxi people do not visit anybody on New Year's Day (He Shaoying 2001: 149 ; Zhang; He 2005: 103).

Among the Masha people living in Weixi County, the men must get the sacred water on New Year's Day; which they hope will bliss fortune to the different activities of the family during the coming year. The following days they visit friends and relatives, celebrate running competitions on the mountains, bull fighting and archery contests (a vestige of the times when hunting was one of their main economic activities), before they start their productive activities again on the eleventh day.

The end of the New Year celebrations, the Chinese Lanterns festival, combines the last festive activities, dragon and lion dances, and some theatrical representations of popular stories, with the first steps in the agricultural cycle of the year, as the Milao Festival (on the 15th), or the Bangbang Fair, when people display and purchase bamboo and wooden farm tools and winter-blooming flowers, or Baisha Agricultural Fair (on the 20th), when people from different minorities, arriving sometimes from distant lands, gather in Baisha streets, around the old temples. The festival originated in the Ming dynasty, when people made pilgrimage to the first place where the Mu kings established their government, to burn incense in front of the Buddha images. The climax of the festival marks the end of the New Year and the beginning of the agricultural activities (He Shaoying 2001: 151). Other agricultural fairs are Longwang miao, celebrated the 15th of the Third Month in the Longwang Temple, that attracts people from all northwest of Yunnan, and Mule and Horse Fair, usually held during one week in the seventh month, when mule, horse and cattle are exchanged, as well as some of the famous products of Lijiang. According to their legends, it was established by the first post-flood ancestor who decided to copy the horse fairs celebrated in Heaven. Naxi horses have been very famous along the history. One of their most important exchange and tribute items, were usually exchanged to traders arriving from distant lands or sent to the emperors as tribute (He Shaoying 2001: 154). Before the beginning of the agricultural cycle, two other important ceremonies are performed: to receive the No spirits of the cattle, when the people of the family changes the old contents of the No spirits basket, and to worship the God of Grain, a ritual held at village level just before starting the agricultural cycle of the year, when one of the chiefs perform a ritual sowing (He Pinzheng 2003).

Torch Festival and other minor festivals

The Grave Sweeping Festival is celebrated in the first week of April, when thinking that their ancestors return for a visit, they clean their graves and pay homage to them. They believe that frequent homage to ancestors is critical to a successful life. In this day they light incense and present some offerings to them. Green willow branches are set in front of the tombs to mark the arrival of another spring, and on the courtyard gates to welcome back the spirits of the ancestors (Pinso 2006: 44- 46). Ancestors are also worshipped in the Hungry Ghost (or Saimei bozee) Festival, celebrated from the 12th to the 14th of the seventh month, when it is believed that their spirits return for a visit. To welcome them the families put tea, vine and incense at the gate of their houses, with the name of the deceased written in colour papers. After lighting incense and offer them food and drink, the family kowtow before a paper that represents them. In some places they are saluted with firecrackers and hot-air balloons. The second day is the time to send the ancestors' spirits back to their resting place. When darkness gathers, the old-aged folks will light colourful small lamps and set them into the river to float, carrying far away the memory of their ancestors. At night they write their clan names on paper and make sacrifices of fruits and grains to them. These two nights the people prefer to stay at home, to avoid the danger of meeting some of the many roaming spirits outside. At Tsipeu Festival, the 2nd day of the 11th month, married daughters return to their natal homes for feasting the ancestors (Pinso 2006, He Shaoying 2001, Goodman 1997).

The God of Medicine is worshipped on the 5th day of the 5th lunar month, when the weather is hot and dry and the danger to get ill is considered higher. They make a straw puppet that hung on their door to keep away evil spirits, they drink the medicine wine and eat the medicine food (usually containing garlic, considered a potent expeller of devils) and worship the God of Medicine at the hearth (He Pinzheng 2003). In the first days of the sixth month the Talbiug Festival is celebrated, an ancestral festival when the Naxi offer their newly harvested wheat to seek the blessing of the spirits (Pinso: 2006: 98).

The Torch Festival is celebrated the twenty-fifth to twenty-seven day of the sixth month. A festival common to most of the peoples related to the Yi, it is considered the small year among the Naxi. Every village sets a big torch and every family a small one, decorated with fresh flowers, outside the front door and lamp boats are set to float on rivers, to expel out the bad influences from their houses, and to protect the safety of the people and their animals (Outlook 1999: 206). In Weixi the Torch Festival is a ceremony to send off the spirits of their ancestors, and for the roving ghost to leave, the wandering ghost of people who died without descendants, who died a violent death or who died without anyone seeing them (Pinso 2006:104). There are a lot of legends concerning this festival. One of the most popular tells that the Jade Emperor was bored in his celestial palace, and every time he opened his door to see the world, he saw the Naxi people enjoying their happy lives. Enraged he sent one celestial deity to exterminate the people and burn their homes and fields. However, when the celestial envoy knew the happy life of the Naxi he felt he cannot exterminate them, and went back to heaven without fulfilling his task. The Jade Emperor, enraged, killed him. He next sent one more celestial envoy with the same mission who was also struck by the kindness of the Naxi people. But fearing to lose his own life, he had a good idea. He then instructed the Naxi to light torches and during three consecutive nights go outside to let the fires be seen by the Jade Emperor, that in this way would think that his orders were carried on (He Shaoying 2001: 155).

To celebrate the Moon festival, on the 15th of the eight month, the whole family sits in a circle in the courtyard after the evening meal to see the full moon. They eat nuts, pomegranates, apples and moon cakes. It's important for the family to be together, watching the full moon and eating moon cakes, and to keep the tradition of giving fruit, nuts and moon cakes to the neighbors (Pinso 2006: 123-4).

Festivals in Eya Township

"Eya Village is like the open museum of social anthropology" (Miyamoto). Festivals performed in Eya, among the more isolated Naxi communities, reflect the importance of the Naxi to preserve archaic cultural characteristics disappeared elsewhere. After the harvest a Women's Festival is celebrated, especially by the women who are married but have no children or whose children are frequently ill, with family, relatives and lovers, taking an active part in it. As wine and meat are distributed during the festival, it is considered also a lovers festival, which men and women of the same family cannot celebrate in the same place. Usually there is a sponsor that provides the 100 kg of grain and wine and some female helpers. Every night during the festival the people gathers on the three main public spaces, where wine is distributed. Groups of three to five women ingeniously dressed and made up, invite old and young to drink wine. Then everybody sits in their assigned places, and while the women twist hemp thread the young play flutes and sing love and history songs. Then one of the boys leads the others to dance around the fire to the rhythm of his flute, soon boys and girls follow him dancing. When the people rest, they start with polite talks, but wine is served continuously and the girls serve with special care those whom they feel affection for. About midnight the older people and the children leave the scene. Some of the youngsters look for their lovers. Those that have no lovers have a good chance to look for suitable ones. Though this is a feast to look for lovers, the love scenario is not in the public space, but every couple looks for their own place: their home, river banks, caves, etc. (Guo 1998).

This festival lasts several days, starting in the last month of the year until the second month of the following year. The start of the festival is very solemn, but later, the drinking, singing and courtship are very free-mode, without nobody caring if anybody changes lovers at will. There are some legends about the origin of this festival, which reflect a time when the people paired freely and possibly a time when the pairing of the human beings was considered an act that can be imitated in the fertility of the land, the fertility of the women and that of the land considered to be on the same symbolic level. This festival could be related to similar gatherings reported in Old China, as well as those that can be found among other minorities, as the Black Thai of Vietnam (Maspero 1929). It is possible that we find among the Naxi living in Eya the last population following ancient rituals once common to grand part of East Asia, now disappeared elsewhere.

The Feast to Love the Domestic Animals is celebrated in the first days of the last month. During seven days oxen, horses, sheep and pigs are especially well feed, cared and accommodated, and the persons that usually take care of these animals are specially honored. Near a tree, people pray for a good harvest and an increase of their domestic animals. The last day the herders will have a night banquet, when they will exchange their experiences during the year.

The Festival to the God of Waters is celebrated the third day of the third month. When they worship the god of waters they are worshiping the three rivers that cross their territory, and the dragon king who lives in their waters, as they think that the dragon raises his head on this day. The Dongbas will be greeted by the people, and will be asked to pray for their ancestors. The day of the ceremony every family will carry his offerings to the bank of the river. Under the direction of a Dongba everybody will kneel facing the river, burn incense, and kowtow, while the Dongba chant some scriptures asking the God of Water to provide good rain and wind to let the crops grow well. When he has finished each family arrange his offerings to make a great communal banquet. Though only people from eight or nine families are present in the ceremony, later all the people would gather in the river, where they will bath and throw their old clothes to the river, to be carried by the water, meaning that all the dirtiness of every person is carried away, and expressing the best wishes for the coming year (Guo 1998).

CHAPTER 7

Music, Arts, and Literature

Naxi music: The rhythm of life

Lijiang offers a splendid and variegated musical landscape created through the interaction of ethnic, religious, economic, political, and technological factors (Xiu). Among the Naxi music marks the rhythm of life and the relation between men and nature. Through music, men share the sacred beat of nature, ask for the blessing of gods, appease demons and become part of an ideal world characterized by the harmony between man and the surrounding environment, and inside of social life. Music is a vehicle of transcendence. A reflection of the reality created with a cultural purpose that allows human beings to transcend it; an invisible thread that guides the persons along the sacred way of life; it accompanies them from birth, grows with them filling with its cadency their main labour and ritual activities, leaving their body only with the sad elegies of the funeral. The protagonist of labour and leisure, sadness and gaiety, love, marriage and even suicide, music impregnates every moment of Naxi life; from the inner rooms of the house to the public space of alleys and squares. In the fields of everyday work or in the festivals and holidays, music accompanies the Naxi from cradle to death, and beyond it, even to the moment when they reach their ancestors' realm. Music is the sacred world of the Naxi.

The most basic classification of Naxi music divides their compositions between sacred and secular songs. The later, being an integral part of their lives, shows a rich repertoire, with genres that include love songs that can be sung as a dialogue with either one man and one woman or a group, wedding songs, children songs, work songs, mountain songs, dance songs, funeral songs and laments, and "spur-of-the-minute" songs, when the singer uses a short melody appropriate to his or her gender and age group (Rees 2000: 58). While the secular songs share many characteristics with those of neighbouring peoples, the sacred music is the true treasury of the Naxi; it includes, besides the Dongba chants that act as a guideline in all their performances, the primal scream Remeicuo, a primitive song and dance music, the large pacifist elegy Bashixile, that reflects wars and conflicts among tribes and expresses people's desire for peace, and the Dongjing music that allowed the preservation of old music already disappeared in the rest of China (People's: 8 -9).

In Naxi music primitive songs that reflect the awe or happiness of humans living in a simple society share room with complex compositions in which elaborated elegies were performed under rich orchestral accompanying. This rich variety of musical forms and styles reflects Naxi history in the borderlands of powerful civilizations; its growth can be

207

understood following four main periods of development. The first, until the middle of the Tang Dynasty, would be the ancient music created during the periods of nomadic hunting, migration, and intermingling by the Naxi forefathers. The second would be the Nanzhao Period, when the musical tradition of the Naxi was modified by the cultural influence of the three great powers of the time: Nanzhao Kingdom, the Chinese Tang dynasty and the Tibetan Tufan Kingdom. The third period, developed before the Mongol conquest, characterized by relative freedom and war, shows the emergence of musical forms that reflect the origins of the Naxi and the humanity, tribal warfare, rituals to avert disaster and ill fortune, shamanism, divination, nature worship and spirit worship. The fourth is the Mu Period, the 500 year rule of the Mu family, when as a result of the influences of the Mongolian singers and the full-scale introduction of Han and Tibetan cultures, traditional Naxi musical forms underwent dramatic changes, with new forms developed including Bashixile, Confucian religious music, Dongjing music, etc. (He Yunfeng 2004).

Layers of historical development with changes in social mores and religious traditions, created an impressive repertory of folk songs and masterpieces of ritual music used in the Dongba primitive activities, with different tunes adapted to the scope and variety of rituals (People's: 36). Among the best known we have the melismatic, free-rhythm mountain songs called in Naxi *Gguq qil (Guqi)*, with a melancholic character that fits well with a variety of themes. They are sung in the main festivals usually with one singer playing the flute, leading the rest of singers and dancers, or sometimes "as a dialogue song, in which two singers face each other and sing alternately, each feeding off the wordplay of the other" (Rees 2000: 57; Guo 1998). Very popular are the charismatic work songs known as *weimongba*, usually sung by a group of people working together in a field. The owner of the field hires one or two professional singers, that must lead the singing all day long. The rest of the people sing while working, and in their happiness they don't feel tired of their physical efforts. Sometimes if they don't finish the song in the fields, they will go on singing at night around the hearth. Other songs depict vividly the wishes of the people and their hope for a good hunt or a bump harvest. Depicting a dog hunting a deer provides

The road to singing in Dongba characters, from left to right: A person speaking, shouting, laughing, singing, and singing and dancing.

good chances of display their musical art with frequent changes of rhythms and a growing intensity that seems to display the action narrated before the eyes of the people. *Gkwua* is a type of song of historical and ancestral topics, sung by old men at weddings on the day which the girl is sent to the groom's house (Rock 1962: 139). *Ndzer-ts'o* are improvised songs full of allegories, sung at weddings and at the Torch Festival, by groups of boys and girls, often of a suggestive nature. The girl being the flower and the boy the bee, or the girl being the snow

209

and the boy the juniper tree on which the snow rests; the latter melts and becomes lost in the juniper (Rock 1962: 325). Of a romantic character are songs that narrate the tragic love of faithful lovers, always ending in the suicide of both them. *T'khi* is a type of song that often relates the bitterness of life, sung in the mountains by lonely travelers (Rock 1962: 433). *Za-za-tso* is sung at funerals of old people or married couples in general, with mourners forming a circle around a night fire holding hands, the leader gently stepping forward and backward, singing a phrase which is repeated by the others, who follow also in the dance (Rock 1962: 499).

Remeicuo singing to drive the spirits away

Remeicuo (also called *arere*) is one of the most primitive singing and dancing traditions which still exists on the earth (People's: 40). An old primeval composition that comes directly from the combination of music and dance, in which the multiple vocal parts enharmonic intervals create a simple beauty (People's: 28). In Naxi "remei" are a kind of demons who attack the corpses of the dead, eat their flesh and drink their blood, "cuo" means "dance". Remeicuo is to use singing and dancing to drive these demons away, usually performed during the night of the funeral by people from different ages and genders in the courtyard of the deceased person. There are no limits to the number of people that can join the dance, as it is considered that the more people dancing the more effective the performance will be (People's: 19). It is thought that originally it was only a dance with the music composed later by Arenmi, inspired by the laments of an old eagle, hungry and lonely, and the mountainous landscapes around Baidi (Outlook 1999). The simplicity and primitiveness of this song point to an old stage of Naxi social development, when living as nomads, they leave their dead to feed wild animals (Guo 1998).

During the dance friends and relatives hold hands, sing and dance slowly around a fire in a clockwise direction, sometimes under the guidance of a Dongba priest. The songs are sung without musical instrumentation. It is a polyphonic two-part song in which the men sing together with a grave voice, and the women answer them with soft and clear voice, all intermingling laments in their songs; suddenly the men use powerful words to drive away the demons and the women cry in loud voice. Singing, the family and friends of the dead remember his past life. Putting emphasis in his main feats they express their sadness at his passing away. After singing and dancing nine times for the male dead and seven times for the female, everybody moves their hands and jumps into the air four times. It is boorish, of primitive simplicity, and powerful. This music comes from fear and expresses the desire to exorcise fear (People's: 20-23); it was originated from the primitive consciousness that singing and dancing are useful to keep away the unsafe factors of the life and to secure a safe existence (Xuan 1999).

Bashixile, a pacifist tragedy

Bashixile, or the music of Baisha, is a large composition with an episodic story told with wind and string instruments, at least 700 years old. "Probably the single most famous

211

indigenous musical form of the Naxi" (Rees 2000: 65). Bashixile, one of the world's earliest musical compositions, was composed to commemorate the tragic love of the Dragon Princess and a Pumi prince; it is a cry against the horrors of war and expresses the people's desire to live peaceful lives with freedom of marriage.

Long time ago the King Mutian of Lijiang, desiring to annex some of the Pumi territories in Muli devised the strategy of forge an alliance marrying his daughter, Princess Dragon, with the Pumi heir prince. The young couple lived happily for some time. One year the king, feigning sickness, called his daughter back to Lijiang with the idea of attract also her husband and to kill him. Dragon Princess arrived first, and quickly learned about the wicked plans of her father. Thinking of a way to warn her husband of the impending disaster, she spent the whole night writing a letter to him, that she hid in the collar of her favourite dog, asking the animal to go back home. When the prince received these news, he immediately arranged his troops and left for Lijiang, without knowing that news of his expedition were leaked and that the King Mutian was waiting for him ambushed in Jade Dragon Mountain. The Pumi army and generals were completely defeated, with the prince killed in the battle. On the battleground corpses made mountains and blood made rivers. When King Mutian found the letter and knew what his daughter had written, decided to punish her locking her without food or water in an island in the middle of the lake until she died (Outlook 1999: 410).

This narration is followed by the performance, which can be divided in the following sections: *Sudu* or elegy to the god of life. *A letter* describes the plot of the history narrated above. In the song *Sansiji*, which means blood flowing like a river, the sadness for the lost of human lives reaches its climax. In *Meimiwu* (goddess crying from heaven) the Dragon Princess receive the news of the ambush and the death of her husband. She is struck with such a great grief that she jumps into Yuhu Lake and drowns herself[22]. *Aliligejipai* is a very sad song sung to release the souls of the soldiers who have been killed in the battle. As the Naxi believe that all disasters are caused by demons, they dance the primitive melody called *Duocuo* to overcome the demons and their evil influences. In the *Kancuo* section, singing and dancing, the performers use arrows to conquer the demons responsible for war. The composition ends with *Mubu,* a long elegy which expresses the people's sadness at war and a desire for future peace. This long musical composition conveys the idea that people's life is precious and war is cruel and wasteful; that battles should not happen and people's real desire is for peace.

In Bashixile instruments play the main role leading the singing and dancing. An orchestra is usually composed of eight musicians, with two of them playing *bili* (horizontal flute), and the other six playing *lengzibili* (vertical flute), *bobo flute, sugudu lute, zheng* bells, *erhuang* and *huqin.* When playing, the musicians are arranged from the young to the elderly. When they are singing they do not dance. When they are dancing they do not sing. After the Qing Dynasty, due to the influence of Han culture, this composition came to be used only at funerals and rituals for worshipping ancestors (People's: 20-22).

---

[22] As in many folk legends there are substantial variations in the plot narrated.

Sacred sounds of Dongba Music

Most of the Dongba religious performances consist in a long chant of their sacred scriptures. Their role as mediators between the world of the humans and the realm of the spirits is unfolded through the aid of ritual music and dance. Chanting is an essential way of expressing the holy texts, and composes an important part of sacrificial activities. The climax of their ceremonies, the request for power that enable the Dongbas to place themselves in a central position, is reached through the transformative effects of music and dance, as they expect to obtain miraculous strength from the magical incantation in song and dance. As music is an indispensable element of every ceremony, it is a necessary study in all Dongba priests' education. Dongba music has three functions: To please the spirits, to delight people so that neither the audience nor the practitioner feels boredom or exhaustion in a long ceremony, and to summon ghosts for pacification and the expulsion of evil. As Lijiang scholar Yang Zenglie says, "People believe that when a Dongba chants scriptures, his voice must be sonorous and pleasing to be heard by the spirits in heaven, the ancestors far away, men on earth, and ghosts in the underworld" (Rees 2000: 55).

The relation of Dongbas with gods and spirits is expressed through their songs, which would be different according to the ceremonies performed and the geographical background of the Dongba involved, with five main musico-religious traditions that would correspond with the ethno-geographical regions the Naxi inhabit. The texts must follow the scriptures proper to every ceremony, and the melody

214

chosen to accompany it, of the more than thirty types of melodies, is applied according to the custom, and passed down from one generation to the next. The rhythm of the chants changes according to its purpose: Those for inviting and sacrificing to spirits and ancestors are smooth-flowing and respectful in mood; those for suppressing and driving out ghosts are louder, more vigorous in rhythm and very aggressive; and those for narrating long legends, tend to be of steady rhythm and often narrow melodic range (Rees 2000: 55). Scriptures are accompanied by the monotonous rhythm of the small drum and the bell; with dance following the long recitations as a musical apotheosis in which wild and sonorous musical instrumentation lead the steps of the Dongba movements (He Shouying 2001). Dongba scriptures include a lot of information on religious music and dance choreography. The meter and rhythm of their chants have preserved many structures and forms of ancient music, which shows primitive traits common to other tribes of Di-Qiang descent (Wu 1999).

The magical power conveyed in the music is shown in the *hualu* or *dharani*. The principle of its efficacy is based on the fact that to each spiritual being belongs a particular rate of vibration, and this kind of vibration is re-formulated and reproduced as sound in *dharanis*, giving the Dongba power even to annihilate by dissolution the particular element or spirit to whom it belongs; thus chanting *dharanis* Dongbas can compel a spirit to act as he wishes. Their *"ability to chant"* means to possess the ability to use one of the most powerful spiritual weapons (Zamblera).

Musical Instruments

215

The original musical instruments of the Naxi are the Jew's harp, flute, gourd flute or pipe, the *maijiesuo*, *quxiang* pipa and the small, high-pitched flute called the *bobo*. Foreign musical instruments serve as proof of their rich musical history, as the Mongol *sugudu*, a 4-stringed Mongolian lute, even today an essential component in Naxi orchestras. They have also instruments common to Chinese classical music: 2, 3 and 4-string instruments played with plectrum or bow, flutes, drums and gongs as well as instruments of Tibetan origin, especially in religious contexts (Goodman 1997: 138). The most splendid exhibition of musical instruments is displayed during the performances of Dongjing music, when the instrumentation alone is far more diverse than that of all other Naxi performances put together.

The Jew's harp is considered to have the ability to speak, as it can reproduce the different vowels; it has been particularly renowned for its role in courtship, as it is considered capable of express any emotion, happy or sad, or to "talk love." The legendary girl Kamegamiki, the first to perform a love suicide, used this instrument to persuade her lover to assent to a suicide pact (Rees 2000: 61-63). Jew's harp was widely used by herders in the mountains. Its melodic music conveyed a kind of secret language perfectly fit to express feelings and emotions. Joy, sadness, loneliness and amorous passion are conveniently expressed through its music (Outlook 1999: 432). Played by both sexes, two main varieties are commonly seen. The first consists of three bamboo strips with a tongue cut into each strip. The second is a single bamboo strip with a tongue cut and a string attached at either end.

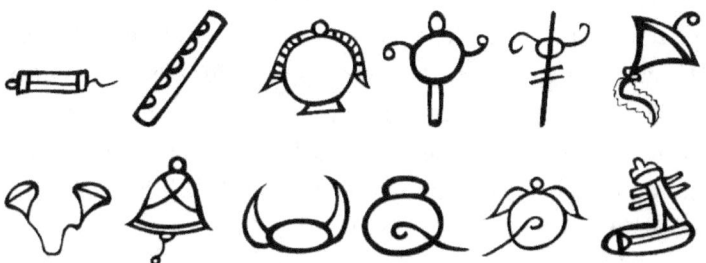

Naxi musical instruments, from left to right: Jews' Harp, flute, drum, hand-drum, flat bells, two bells, bell, horns, conch, ddagula (rataplan), and zither.

The Naxi use nature elements to make perishable musical instruments, among which tree leaves and barley straws are widely used. Any elliptical, smooth-surfaced leaf fresh from its tree may be used to produce music, and it will be discarded after playing. Barley-stalk pipes are made from tender shoots during the spring months, its sound being "particularly associated in the Naxi imagination with springtime and courtship" (Rees 2000: 64-5).

The Dongba also use a variety of percussion instruments. The most common are a large drum beaten with a curved stick, a small rattle drum, a plain cymbals for driving ghosts, a conch shell for inviting deities, and yak horn (Rees 2000: 56; He and He 1999). Other musical instruments used in their rituals include flutes and gourd mouth organ (*hulusheng.*) In the Dongba scripts can be found some musical instruments already disappeared. Because supernatural powers are attributed to musical instruments, there are strict rules as to when they may be played and which Dongba may use them (Rees 2000: 56). The flat bell or single cymbal, called *ds-ler*, is the most precious ceremonial object of a Dongba, who use it when he dances and chants during the ceremonies. When a Dongba dies the *ds-ler* is often passed to his son or grandson; the pieces of cloth attached to it represent the previous owners. Drums of all sizes are also vital to Dongba activities; specially the small hand-held drum, called *dabbalar*, and large drums beaten in important ceremonies.

The exuberance of Dongjing Music

Dongjing music is the most famous artistic activity of the Naxi. Actively promoted as the essence of Naxi musical art in the last years is however a fusion of cultural contents with a strong Chinese influence. According to the legends when Kublai Khan came to Lijiang, in gratitude for the assistance the Naxi gave his army, he left them an orchestra, almost fully outfitted, and a number of musical compositions, which were performed at the Song Dynasty courts[23]. This legend reflects the fact that about the 13th and 14th centuries, some Chinese compositions spread to Lijiang and were quickly accepted by people already passionate about music. It's possible however that Chinese music were brought to Lijiang after the visit to Nanjing of King Mu De, and that these musical styles were preserved in Lijiang as part of the growing influence of Chinese culture and the attraction it had among the upper classes in Naxi society. This Taoist music usually is played in the main hall of a Taoist temple or in the courtyard of a private house. Many famous ancient songs now already lost in China are

---

[23] Enmity between Mongols and Chinese do not blocked the transmission of art and cultural forms.

preserved only in Lijiang. Among them the melodies *Bagua*, compiled in 741 by the Emperor Xuanzong; *The Song of Water Dragon*, played as homage to the goddess Mazu; *The Wave Washing the Sands* of the Tang Dynasty; or *The Sheep on the Hill*, a sacred music of the Yuan Dynasty. The traditional form of musical notation was also lost in China but preserved in the Naxi Ancient Musical Repertoire. The treasure of classical music preserved in Lijiang can be regarded as a "living musical fossil" (People's).

The Dongjing musico-ritual associations, widespread in Yunnan Province from the sixteenth century on, blended Confucian, Taoist, and Buddhist elements in their beliefs and ritual (Rees 2000: 4-6). As they used a version of the *Yuqing Wuji Zongzhen Wenchang Dadong Xianjing* (Transcendent Scripture of the Great Grotto of Wenchang), this full title is commonly reduced for convenience to *Dadong Xianjing*, and later to Dongjing (Rees 2000: 41). Though Dongjing Musical Associations adopted Chinese paraphernalia, they impregnated in the music the sacred meaning of art that permeates Naxi religion and life.

To have a first-hand idea of the environment surrounding Dongjing music in the years before 1949, nothing fits better than the words of Peter Goullart: "The concerts were a unique institution and were so inspiring and interesting that I never failed to attend them. It was wonderful and extraordinary to hear the music which was played during the heyday of the glorious Han and Tang dynasties, and probably during the time of Confucius himself. This musical tradition was one of the most cherished among the Naxi and was zealously transmitted from father to son. A well-to-do Naxi in the city could only be accepted as a real gentleman if he knew this ancient music or was a fully fledged Chinese scholar" (1957: 290).

"When I was in Lijiang sacred concerts were usually held at some rich man's house. At intervals food and drinks were served both to the participants and the guests. The musical sessions were long and arduous but everybody was happy and attentive. The instruments were carefully arranged in a long room, sometimes in the enclosed veranda, and the atmosphere was reverent and definitely religious, with the scent of incense burning in great brass burners."

"There were the old carved frames on which multi-toned bronze bells were hanging in rows. Another frame had rows of chromatic jade pieces in the form of lunettes. A great and sonorous gong was suspended from a tall stand. There was a long *chin* or the prototype of the modern piano lying on a long table. Only very few people knew how to play it. And there were huge standing guitars, smaller *pipas* and several kinds of long and short flutes and pipes."

"The old musicians, all formally dressed in long *gowns* and *makwas*, took their seats unhurriedly, caressing their long white beards. One man acted as conductor. They peered at the score: a flute wailed and one by one other instruments joined in. Although I... cannot describe the music that followed in technical terms. It was majestic and inspiring and proceeded in rising and falling cadences. Then, as a climax, the great gong was struck. I have never heard in China such a deep and sonorous gong: the whole house seemed to vibrate with its velvety waves. Then, rising from their chairs, the elders sang a sacred ode in a natural voice and with great reverence and feeling. Then the symphony continued, with notes of unimagined sweetness, falling like a cascade from the jade lunettes, and giving way to a golden shower of sounds from the chromatic bells. The chords from the great *chin* were like diamonds dropped into the golden melody, reinforced by a stopped diapason. Never was there any dissonance or retreat from harmony... To a Western ear it might have appeared somewhat monotonous, but actually there was no repetition. It was only that the theme was unfolding in rhythmic waves of sound into which new motives were constantly introduced. It was a recital of the cosmic life as it was unfolding in its grandeur, unmarred by the discordant wails and crashes of petty human existence. It was classical, and timeless. It was the music of the gods and of a place where there is serenity, eternal peace and harmony" (Goullart 1957: 293).

The performance of the ritual Dongjing session follows a pattern already familiar to the reader. During the three or more days required to perform a complete ceremony, the members would chant, and read their way through a fixed set of religious scriptures starting from the first character of the first volume until they reached the last character of the last volume. As in the Dongba ceremonies the ritual was directed by the chief ritual officiant and second ritual officiant, which were men chosen by their fellow members for their moral uprightness and, most important, for their intimate knowledge of the scriptures, ritual protocol, and music. The session was performed in a sacred space created around an altar with Chinese symbols and statues of the deities Wenchang and

Guandi[24] elevated on a table, that were visually and spatially differentiated from the worshipers (Rees 2000: 100- 103). The seat positions of the musicians were arranged around eight tables set in front of the altar with one of the eight trigrams written on the cloth hanging over the front of each table. As in the Dongba ceremonies these deities were called in the *Rite of Opening the Altar,* empowered through the *Complete Formal Invocation, Transcendent Scripture,* and *Complete Divine Spells and* sent off with the aid of the *Wenchang Rite of Lighting a Lamp* (Rees 2000: 201). Parallelisms between Dongjing music and Dongba ritual suggest the existence of an older ritual procedure over which new creations were performed, an older conscience of the relationship between art and well-being and of the power of art to expel bad states of conscience.

This very refined and sweet music can effectively relieve uneasiness of body and mind and bring good health to people. Every relatively big Naxi village in Lijiang has its own band with musicians from varied strata and trades (He and He 1999: 106). Dongjing associations were an active factor in the creation of local social identities, becoming important in the definition of regional social structures and relationships that took shape through the performance of religious rituals designed to be sumptuous, solemn, and exclusive (Rees 2000: 99); rituals that reinforced Naxi elites' proficiency in Han cultural forms, and thus their differentiation from ordinary commoners around them, which included to move with stately decorum, and to practice an elaborately choreographed set of

---

[24] Wenchang is the literary god of the Chinese, Guandi the military god, being both civil and military the two spheres of government in classical China.

kowtows and bows to their gods and to one another. Corporate status was reinforced by their communal ownership of instruments and ritual paraphernalia (Rees 2000: 100- 103). Four main festivals were celebrated annually to honour Wenchang and Guandi. Private ceremonies were also common; especially funerals for Dongjing association members or their relatives (Rees 2000: 47-51). Dongjing associations were governed by the chief ritual officiant, which organized the ceremonies, called members together, and directed the music. The manager prepared everything for the ceremonies and supervised the ritual program; the disciplinarian watched for infringements of the rules of behavior during ceremonies and meted out penalties; the financial manager looked after property, rent, and other financial matters and organized food for meetings (Yang Zenglie 1990: 119-120 in Rees 2000: 113).

Contemporary orchestras have not resuscitated their ritual and religious content; turning their music instead in a more secular direction, which allow them to play their music for entertainment on a regular basis, slowly endowing this music with a strong Naxi rather than class identity (Rees 2000: 189). The Dayan Ancient Music Orchestra, whose director is Xuan Ke, has become renowned around the world. There are also another 21 ancient Naxi music orchestras scattered throughout the town of Lijiang and its surrounding countryside (People: 9-10). The present revival of Dongjing music in Lijiang can help understand the ways the Naxi developed to recreate their own culture, including foreign elements they consider interesting and the search of new ways to define their ethnic identity before the Chinese Han and the global audience that reach their lands by means of the tourism

223

and international mass media. The transformation of Dongjing music from a social distinguished activity to an ethnic marker helps understand the recent history of the Naxi and other minorities in the second half of the 20th century.

Dance of the Naxi: the road to ecstasy

To try to determine the origin of dance among the Naxi would carry us to the academic debates about the origin of dance in human culture. Traditions still alive among the Naxi, as those regarding the *remeicuo* dance, suggest that in the past people could have mourned their deceased relatives dancing in a circle, maybe around a shaman who performing a set of more elaborated steps, tried to exorcise the spirits of death, as both *llubhu* shamans and Dongba priests are described as dancers in old Naxi documents and some of their most important ceremonies are related to sickness and death. Today dance is present in Naxi everyday life and their more solemn ceremonies.

Dongba dance

Dance is a vehicle to trance. Though it seems that not all Dongba priests reached trance during their ceremonies, a situation commonly associated with the task of the *llubhu* shamans, it is possible that in former times trance and altered states of conscience were common during their long ceremonies. In fact, some of the magical skills associated with trance, as the licking of red hot iron rods, the piercing with knives or walking on red charcoal have been reported among them. Dance is an important part of the religious ceremonies of the Dongba, an integral part of their rituals. When they are called upon to send a recently deceased soul on its long, arduous path to the afterlife, to exorcise a ghost, or to perform sacrifices to the Gods; ritual dance is invariably involved: hours of intense physical activity under the sound of drums and cymbals, that can invest the Dongba with the power required to act as a mediator in the ceremony, or to directly confront the devils and expel them.

In Naxi dance there are sixty sets of movements, usually performed accompanied by percussion instruments with a great degree of freedom, classified under several categories,

Cards showing some of the movements of a Dongba dancing

such as dance of animals, dance of sacrifice, dance of rivalry, dance of gods, etc. The Dongba priest changes from one style to the other in the curse of one ceremony, as the dances often enact legendary stories told in the scriptures, and he must play the roles of the people, gods and animals involved – tigers, horses, birds, etc.-, reflecting a form of shamanistic animism that require movements precise and physically demanding (Duncan 2010a). The scripture named *The origin of dance* explains that in the origin dance was taught by gods and was directly modeled on animals (He Shangli 2000: 54). Other scriptures provide a detailed description of every kind of dance; the number, position and movements of the dancers, accompanying music and musical instruments, all is perfectly registered. For the Dongbas, every kind of dance has a different function: To invite the gods, to send them off, to suppress the devils, etc. Each of the steps of their long ceremonies is performed in a particular way, following a fixed set of steps that the would-be Dongba must learn during his formative years. Flowers dance, peacock dance, and white crane dance are used for flattering the deities, while the sword dance, Garuda dance and dragon dance, are performed for driving away demons (He and He 1999: 101). In the Dance of Dongba Shiluo, which must be performed after the death of a Dongba priest, the narrative dance includes: The Birth of Dongba Shiluo, Dongba Shiluo learns to walk, Dongba Shiluo subdues the demons, Searching the corpse of Dongba Shiluo, etc. (Outlook 1999: 463).

Dances can be classified according to their function, as funeral dances, dances to ask for longevity, to worship the Shu spirits, the wind demons, or divinatory dances. A common characteristic of Dongba dances is that in all of them a ritual fight against the devils or offended spirits is enacted, with good vanquishing bad, and light vanquishing darkness (He Shaoying 2001: 134). This battle is clearly shown in the fact that when they dance they must hold in their hands at least three tools: a bell that represents the sun, always held in the left hand, a hand drum that represents the moon, and a knife, usually in the right hand. The bell and drum are used to play out the rhythm of the dance, and to scare off evil spirits or welcome beneficial

226

ones (Duncan 2010a). Pitchforks, weapons, bows and arrows are sometimes held in the hands while dancing.

Dongba pictographs were used to record dozens of classical dance in dance notations called *chamu*. Not only they are the only existing works written in ancient characters, exclusive for dance, they are also the earliest dance notation found in the world. These records on classical Naxi dance are valuable and significant for studying the birth and development of dance and the source of religious dance. Experts believe that "Dongba Dance Score is the most ancient and perfect dance score" (He and He 1999: 99). The *chamu* dance notations provide a complete description of the dance experience, with the dance ground, dancers position, steps, movements, actions, lines and skills of 41 dancing programs in total (He 1987: 41). The dance score in common use at present, called Lhapan Dance Score, was created in the 15th century. Written in their pictographic script, is simple and easy to learn. In the Dance Rules in Offering Sacrifice to Shiluo, an ancient dance book, can be read: "In the olden days, on the fertile and vast land where mankind grew, 360 Dongba had not learned to dance. Upon this time, appeared at the First Sea a tree seedling with leaves thin as hair. This was the Heyibada Tree. On the tree rested the three Victory Gods - the Giant Roc, the Lion, and the Flying Dragon- that learned the method of dance from the Golden Frog that in turn had learned dancing from the Goddess Panzhusamei (the wise and beautiful goddess of music and dance), who lived above 18 levels of the sky. From her came the dance of the 360 Dongba" (Zhao 1987: 90).

Secular dances and communal life

227

Naxi folk dances present some common characteristics and many local variations; as a general rule dances are often accompanied by vocal music. The participants dance and sing simultaneously, usually holding hands and performing a repetitive set of simple steps. They have preserved some very old dances, such as the primitive funeral dance *remeicuo* or the ancient hunting dance *e'rere* that originated in times when the Naxi were still nomad herders. They used to go into the mountains to hunt in the daytime, and danced and sung around bonfires while feasting on the game they had taken at night. *E'rere* is a group dance led by one person, in which between four and five hundred people can take part. It is performed at important festivals or during breaks in field work, especially in the transplanting season. The men sing melodies similar to those sung in pursuit of wild animals, while the women's *"hai, hai, hai,"* sounds like the cry of the animals, forming a magnificent hunting scene (Zhao 1987: 104-5).

Yahali is an ancient dance possibly created in the 14th century; as the name comes from the shout of the cavalry in Kublai Khan's times. Still popular nowadays, men and women, hand in hand in a circle, swing their arms back and forth. The main movement is a step forward on the left foot, close with the right foot and stamp (Zhao 1987: 105). Nowadays, the most famous dance is the celebratory song *Alili*, whose simple movements were developed from a Naxi folk song popular in the Baishuitai region, and which spread within Lijiang County only just before 1949. "Alili" are vocables that begin each verse of the song (Rees 2000: 58). In Lijiang city and other localities, every day at dusk, citizens gather in the main square to enjoy the happy spirit conveyed by the Alili dance.

Clear Chinese influences are perceived in the Lusheng Dance and Flute dance, when the instrument player leads the dance in the center of the dance ground. Animal dances as Playing Dragon, Lion Dance and Unicorn Dance, can be considered basically Chinese with slight Naxi influences (Zhao 1987: 106-9).

Naxi Sacred Art

Every Dongba is an artist, a person able to draw with precision the books that would lead him along each ceremony,

Naxi hieroglyphic dance notation. Goddess Lamu dance. "When performing the goddess Lamu dance, shake three times the handdrum, jingle once the flat bell, rock the body three times to the left, and then three times to the right; turn about to the left once, and then to the right once". Ge Agan. 1992

the paintings of gods and demons required for the set up, and the assorted variety of miscellaneous paintings, mouldings and carvings. Relation between art and the sacred realms of the existence could have been known by the ancestors of the Naxi, maybe even before they started their southward migrations, as wood paintings with a religious use have been found near their ancient territory in northwest China and among peoples related with them. Of the Naxi artistic manifestations, maybe the better known are the Dongba paintings and the temple frescoes; the Dongba paintings are an indigenous Naxi art, while the frescoes were part of a multiethnic project in which the Naxi artists had only a minor role.

Dongba Paintings

Dongba pictographic writing is a painted writing. Each of the pictographs of a text must be carefully painted by the Dongba, sometimes being even coloured to add esthetic value. It is a beautiful combination of both language and painting used to tell the myths and stories included in their ceremonies (He Shangli 2000: 53). Every Dongba priest is a painter used to express through drawing the basic concepts of his religion. Lacking a centralized organization, well-known artists among the Dongba priest developed different regional styles or artistic schools, in which gods, ancestors and deities showed interesting differences, while Dongbas of lesser artistic capacity would follow their master's steps. The art of the Dongba priests extends beyond the field of pictographic writing. Images of gods and devils needed to set the stage where their ceremonies are performed are usually painted by themselves. Pictorial representations of the gods including wood painting, paper painting and scroll painting, are in general made by Dongba at odd times and kept in store, to be brought along to the ritual site when required (He and He 1998: 140).

There are five kinds of Dongba painting:

1. Wooden slab painting (k'o-byo) is one of the oldest Dongba artistic traditions. Originally were painted with a

bamboo pen, without colour, later works are beautifully coloured images of Dongba deities. In most of their ceremonies a number of slab paintings with the portraits of the main gods must be displayed on the sacrificial spot, usually inserted into the ground. With a height of 50-60 cm and a width of about 10 cm, they can be easily carried to the ceremonial ground, and stored after the ceremony for posterior use. Before a ceremony the Dongba must select a number of these paintings. After finishing, those representing demons and ghosts must be destroyed, while those representing gods are carried back home to be used in future ceremonies (Guo 1999). Wooden slabs paintings function as reverence to gods and dispelling the evil spirits, they usually have a fixed design. Its shape reflects a frog head and a snake tail, two of the main elements of the Naxi symbolic universe. Those representing gods have a triangular end and those representing demons a trunked end. Each slab has a main painting of the deity to whom it is dedicated, and around him, auspicious designs, conchs and animals related with him, as well as a short Dongba text to please him. In the wooden slabs for worshipping the gods of nature the animals painted represent the animals caught and killed by the people, meaning that through the ceremony, they are returning them back to nature and apologizing to nature. Some Dongbas can draw the designs of demons and deities of the slab paintings without a model or sketch, adding later the colours that the tradition assigns each deity (He Zhiwu 1992; He and He 1999: 50).

2. Painting with bamboo brush used in the front page of the Dongba books, occasionally reaching an exquisite craftsmanship.

231

3. Paper-slab paintings. Handy, they are easy to use in varied rituals, when the main deities and demons of Dongba tradition are displayed in the place where the ceremony is performed. Paper paintings are also used in card divination and other divinatory rituals, in which the images of the Dongba deities would lead the Dongba along his interpretive road. Cards are painted also to exorcise ghost and demons, and will be used during exorcist rituals or funerals. Sometimes the funeral cards depict scenes related to only a section of the complex ritual that would finish with the arrival of the deceased soul to the ancestor's realm. On the other side, propitiatory cards with the images of Naxi main deities constitute the altar on which offerings will be done to them (He Zhiwu 1987: 39; Guo 1999: 63; He and He 1999: 63).

4.   Sacred rolled paintings stored as the Tibetan *thangkas*, are colorful paintings that convey happiness and respect, in which the main Dongba deities are represented: Supreme gods, war gods, gods of the five cereals, being the most common the scrolls of their guardian gods, easily unfolded and hung before performing their ceremonies. *Thangkas* of Dongba Shiluo are used in almost all Dongba ceremonies. Easy to carry to the ceremonial ground, they are unfolded before the start of the ritual, and pick up after it finish. Dongba Shiluo is usually depicted seated between two elephants on a lotus throne, a clear Buddhist symbology. He has usually a green body; the color associated with the south in Naxi cosmology. Above him are depicted the gods of the five elements, two dragons standing on his shoulders, his horse, somewhere below the throne, and some of his disciples. "These images are not intended for decorative or meditative purposes;

Wooden slab painting.
Yunnan Provincial
Museum

they are "living representations" of the deities the priests invoke during the ceremony. As they represent the higher gods, these images must always be placed at a high level in the ritual space, usually above the altar" (Mathieu and Ho 2011: 140).

5. Long scroll paintings used in funerals. The most beautiful of the Dongba paintings is the big scroll known as the "Road to Heaven," an original piece of art-work specially used in funeral ceremonies, 30 centimeters in width and 20 meters in length, where about 300 deities, demons and saints are carefully painted, as well as about 100 species of birds and animals. Showing a mysterious world of demons and deities; it could be regarded as a magnificent reflection of the Naxi mythology of death. It has three major contents: The divine land, earthly world and hell. It is used for "releasing the souls of the departed" rituals in the funerals, with the Dongba priest helping the soul of the deceased avoid the torments of hell. This kind of painting is regarded as the longest ancient scroll painting; "it offers an

233

insight into Naxi morality, ideas of sin and personal responsibility" (Roosevelt: 9). During the ritual, the Dongba "place a scroll at the head of the coffin and unroll it in a northeastern direction, pointing to the land of the ancestors" (Roosevelt: 3), and chant the words of the scripture entitled *Guiding the Road Close to the Gods* in order to effectively guide the soul of the departed through the various realms of hell and rebirth until he or she reaches the final release in the realm of the gods (Li Xi 2001), where "everything is peaceful and beautiful and there is no more fighting or sin" (Roosevelt: 9).

The ceremonial texts recall the journey to the afterlife made by the founder of their religion, Dongba Shiluo, and the multitude of sacrifices offered to demons and gods along the way. With the help of the Dongba the departed soul journeys on the road first traveled by Shiluo in the six realms of existence and possible rebirth, passing through the places of torments and suffering in the realm of hell, the realm of the demons and hungry ghosts, the realm of the beasts, the human world, and the land of the titans or *asuras* until they finally reach the peaceful realm of the gods (Mathieu and Ho 2011: 178).

Dongba art is reborn in the work of Naxi modern artists who incorporate their main themes in the composition of paintings of different styles. Some of them are scholars with a perfect knowledge of Dongba pictographs that work in the conscience of the disappearance of their use (Debon 1999). A popularization and vulgarization of this sacred art have been a consequence of the development of the tourism industry in Lijiang and the commoditization of the most visible aspects of Naxi culture. Every kind of objects, wherever made, can be transformed into suitable samples of Naxi art with the painting or engraving of some colorful free-style Dongba pictographs.

Baisha Frescoes

One of the most remarkable icons of Naxi artistic heritage are the Baisha Frescoes, a set of Ming Dynasty religious paintings that decorate the walls of the main temples of Baisha, the cradle of Naxi culture and the ancestral home of the Mu kings. Heavily influenced by Chinese culture, the Mu kings invited some famous painters from China and Tibet, and local artists both Naxi and Bai to decorate their favorite temples. The original frescoes were distributed in more than 15 Buddhist and Taoist monasteries and palaces. The oldest being painted in 1385 -the start of an artistic tradition that lasted more than 200 years. The frescoes reflect the border spirit of Lijiang; their contents are representative of the coexistence of various religions in a unique Naxi culture, where Chinese Buddhist and Taoist influences, Tibetan Lamaist and local traditions are blended. Nowadays there are still 53 frescos preserved, covering a total area of 171 square meters, of which the best painted are those of Dabaoji Palace of Baisha and of Dajue Palace of Shuhe.

Dabaoji Palace was built in 1582; its name refers to the profound law of Mahayana Buddhism that teaches believers how to acquire Buddhist law and values and accumulate good deeds. Inside it, three big and superb frescoes decorate the three main walls and nine smaller the corners between them. The fresco on the front wall, with an area of 367 x 498 cm (18,2 sqm), is the biggest and the most representative, whose subject

235

matter is derived from the scene of a Amitayus Preaching Conference, where a group of saints is listening to the teachings of Amitayus. Altogether more than one hundred deities are painted in this fresco. At the upper part there is a row of 18 Buddhist saints, on the two flanks images of Taoist gods, and on the lower part images of three Buddhist Marshals in the center with four Heavenly Kings on their two sides. The fresco painted in the center of the north wall, a little smaller, is a representation of a Buddhist sutra that tells how all suffering creatures could get rid of their miseries if they call the name of Avalokitesvara, who would come to help them immediately. The disasters and calamities that can be suffered are depicted in vivid details, with the classical themes of Buddhist lore perfectly identifiable: "seeing the sufferings of the king," "death before the torture," "the breaking of the sword," "confronting the bandits on the road," "meeting the tiger in the forest," and "fire disaster of the lotus pond." In Dajue Palace the frescoes mainly describe the scene of Boddishatvas and other Buddhist saints, as well as some Taoist motifs (Li Xi 1999: 17). The most outstanding feature of the Lijiang frescoes is the integration of painting skills of different nations. Their unique blending of religious faiths, cultural themes, ethnic types and artistic styles have become a precious resource for studying the history of ethnicity, art and religion in the area (Zhang and He 2005: 61; Yang 1999).

Variety of Naxi Sculpture

If the sacred concept of life is present in all manifestations of Naxi art, this is especially prominent in the sculpture. The most common sculptures of the Naxi are the  Dongba priests use in some ceremonies. With a size of around 10-15 cm, made of clay or dough, they represent Shu nature spirits, deities and demons. Being their religious carvings and moldings the crucial elements in some of their most important ceremonies, and at the same time, receptacles of gods, demons and dead souls, its making is invested of all the sacred power of the Dongba tradition. The *duoma*, with its simple form and perishable material, are the suitable place where the spirits that cause sickness must be sent and expelled or destroyed. After the ceremony, all the figurines will be thrown away, dough figurines usually being eaten by dogs. During the curse of the ritual, figurines of deities are put at the sacred place while figurines of ghosts are put at the ghost's village (He and He 1999: 68).

The celestial realms of the Road to Heaven, by He Zhiben

Carved wood figurines representing the dead, used in some funerals, require the Dongba to have knowledge of different arts and artistic techniques. They also convey, as the *duoma* figurines in other rituals, the power to become an ideal lodge to the soul of the deceased. Put in a cave near the village, a sacred place in their local geography, they symbolize the travel of the proper soul to the ancestors' lands, and maybe, at the same time, the return of the Sv life god to the womb (cave) of Mother Nature. Sometimes the Dongba priests carve wood figurines as durable substitutes for the clay or dough figurines.

A non indigenous tradition can be found in the sculptures of the numerous temples belonging to the Buddhist, Taoist and Lamaist faiths, where the main deities and saints of their traditions are carefully carved, as well as many architectural elements of the temples' structure, decorated with designs of flowers, phoenixes, dragons, birds and other symbolic motifs. These decorative styles are present also in most of the Naxi traditional houses, especially in the richest houses and palaces of Lijiang city, where the main gates, beams, doors and windows are embellished with auspicious symbols.

Masterworks of Naxi literature

Most of the works of the Naxi literature can be found in the Dongba manuscripts, the encyclopedia of traditional Naxi culture that contains their myths and legends, epics, folk-tales, love stories, animal fables, didactic stories, and the secret formula for addressing the gods or casting inhibitory spells on demons (Goodman 1997: 125-6).

The most important myths of the Naxi are: *The Descend of Man*, also called *Creation of the world* or *The migration*, *The War between White and Black* and the romantic narration *Lubanlushao*. These three narratives provide a mythic account of the main characteristics of the Naxi people. *The Migration* establishes the divine origin of the ancestors of the Mu Kings and the Naxi; *The War between White and Black* justifies the right of the Naxi to govern over the conquered original inhabitants of these lands, as the possessors of higher moral principles. *Lubanlushao* relates the origin of the love suicides so common among the Naxi.

The Descend of Man is the mythic history of the ancestors of the Naxi people and of their Mu Kings; it narrates the origin of the Naxi as a result of the marriage of Congrenlien, the only survivor to the flood, and Cunhongbaobai, daughter of the god of heaven and provider of the grains and agricultural techniques. In the myth, sound and breath transformed themselves into a pair of eggs, one white and one black, which transformed themselves also in the ancestors of the human beings and demons. After some generations of human beings, Congrenlien and his five brothers and six sisters paired between themselves, annoying the gods. Congrenlien knew of the coming flood and the way to avoid it, becoming the only human being that survived it. He wandered alone looking for a woman to marry. In his first encounter with two goddesses, he chooses, against the advice of the gods, the good looking one, that was unable to give birth to human beings. He wandered alone again and met with Cunhongbaobai, the daughter of the heavenly god Zilao Apu, who had been promised to a family of deities she disliked. Love surged between them and Cunhongbaobai took Congrenlien with her to her heavenly home. Though she hid her human boyfriend, her father discovered him. Before allowing the marriage of a heavenly princess with a human being, Zilao Apu probed the abilities of Congrenlien, asking him to put fire to a field, to cut the trees, to sow the seeds, and harvest the grain, tasks that Congrenlien completed only with the magic help of Cunhongbaobai. When he thinks his tests are over, he must survive a dangerous hunting expedition and a fishing evening. At the end he must get three drops of a tigress' milk. The couple then leaves their heavenly home and go down to earth with the five grains and the domestic animals as dowry, in their way they are harassed by the weather deity to whom Cunhongbaobai was formerly promised, but they appease him with some offerings. After a little time on earth they have three sons, who cannot speak until their father makes the Sacrifice to Heaven to honor their heavenly ancestors. These three sons are the ancestors of the Tibetan, Naxi and Bai peoples.

In the *War between White and Black* is described the fighting between the tribe of Dong and the tribe of Shu. Dong is the white people, symbol of the light and of the positive virtues of the human beings. Shu is the black people, symbol of the darkness and of the negative characteristics of devil spirits. This myth describes two worlds set apart. One characterized by the light and white colour, the domain of the Dong family, and the other as the domain of the black spirits of the Shu family. In a moment, a communication is opened between the black and the white worlds, and the heirs of the princely families of both worlds engage in a dice game. The white heir lost and the black heir only demands of him to create light in his domains,

Main characters in Naxi mythology, from left to right: Congrenlien, the first post-flood ancestor, other representation of Congrenlien; Caolequ, a descendant of Congrenlien; Cunghongbaobai, the divine mother of all human beings. Zilaoapu, the great god of Heaven, her father.

promising to pay him with a treasury of gold and silver. The white heir feigns to fulfill his promise, but he flies from the black world carrying treasures. The black heir pursues him but is killed in a tramp set up by his enemy. The chief of the black Shu clan swears to avenge the death of his son killing the white Dong heir, but only through the charms of a beautiful shaman can they entice him to the Shu territory, killing him. When the Dong chief receives news of his son's death, he arranges a powerful army that, commanded by Yuma and Duoge celestial generals defeats the Shu and exterminates them. The myth is permeated of a dualism prone to multiple interpretations: from the psychological complexity of the human mind to the geographical wandering of the forefathers of the Naxi; from a symbolism of the victory of the Dongba religion (with its Bon influences) over the indigenous animism to the victory of the Naxi invaders over the primitive inhabitants of these lands.

Lubanlushao is a tragic romantic story that tells how in the past boys and girls herded their goats in the alpine meadows enjoying a merry life of singing, dancing and free loving. Their parents went up to call them down, but they did not agree to end their merry life and remained in the pastures. At the end, the boyfriend of Kamakugichi is taken home by his parents, and the girl, not desiring to live without him, hangs herself from a tree in the mountain. When the boyfriend discovers her corpse, her spirit entices him to follow her to the land of the death.

The rich mythology of the Naxi has preserved hundreds of myths relating the origin of all what exists in this world. Especially important is *The Origin of Medicine,* that narrates how many animals and plants became impregnated with the medicine of immortality, from where humans can collect it to cure ill persons. *The origin of the horse* or *The origin of the tiger* must be chanted in ceremonies when the horse or the tiger are summoned; others, such as *The origin of the sun and moon,* were preserved in their oral tradition. They have also myths that narrate the relationship between man and nature, man and woman, and different aspects of Naxi society. To have an idea of the richness of their mythology, it will suffice to know that during Dongba ceremonies, every time that a new object is introduced, a new deity talked about, or a new ancestor summoned, his history must be related to justify his power to act as is requested in the ceremony. In the Dongba scripts, we can find not only their main myths, but also a wide collection of legends, folk-tales, poems and proverbs. "For everything in this world the Naxi have an origin story at hand; for natural phenomena, for fabricated objects of both ritual and everyday use, for technological achievements, for social institutions and for religious activities. These stories tell us why things are as they are, and they attest to their right of existence" (Oppitz 1998: 7).

Out of the Dongba tradition a rich variety of folk literature has been orally preserved and transmitted, with contents reaching all aspects of human existence. Legends describe their history and the geographical accidents of their territory. Folk tales not related to the sacred and religious sphere include romantic and tragic stories, custom and educative tales, and adventures of orphans, dragons, ogres or clever personages. Sometimes the protagonists are heroes and important personages of the past, as *The origin of Mulaoye*; sometimes the tale shows how the demons were subdued, as in *Two sisters*; or they narrate humorous stories, as those of the clever Ayidan, always striving to help his poor country-fellows. They have also a rich variety of tales of special scenery; legends of war and resistance against the enemies, and tales of ethic and moral principles. Every kind of songs, fables, riddles and proverbs complete the rich panorama of Naxi literature. Not so interesting to the outside reader are the numerous Naxi writers who were successful in the literary world of the Chinese, a result of their early adoption of their educative system (Outlook 1999).

Popular songs are almost daily used by Naxi people. Most of them have a joyful tone, and are related to their everyday behavior and life cycle. Love, festivals and other merry occasions are usually accompanied by songs, and their main productive activities are frequently done under the tune of labour songs: songs to be sung while weaving, before leaving to hunt, milking the she-yak, etc. Labour songs act as a charm, sung in the hope that the aim of their action is properly achieved, the cloth successfully weaved, the hunt hunted; and they also act as educative tools, reminding the proper way to do every productive activity. They have also great value as tools that provide psychological links among the members of the community.

Naxi proverbs are an important educative resource; their apparently simple message contains the basic instructions of the ethic and moral education for the people. Modern collections of proverbs include a systematic exposition of their worldview. In one of the most famous editions, the 200 traditional proverbs selected are arranged in sections that cover a wide spectrum of educative content: aim high (no obstacle can stop a fine horse), take care of environment (don't pick the young fruit of the tree), go with the seasons (wheat is not ripe until the weather is hot), respect relatives and friends (a mother's call resounds in all directions), keep a family by hard work (shedding nine drops of sweat for a grain of wheat), on self-cultivation (the Golden Sand River stores gold but flows in silence), plain living (seeing the river yet beyond reach, one has no water to make tea), life disciplines (toads should not aspire to consume the flesh of a swan), and national pride, consisting on the words from Congrenlien, their first post-flood ancestor (Guo and Zheng 1998).

Epilogue

The world is changing very quickly. In the last decades ethnic groups that have succeeded in developing their original cultures according to their own wishes and interests, have been reached by the globalizing wave that floods our planet. If the world is changing, the Chinese world where the Naxi live is changing even more quickly. The 20th century and the first years of the 21st century are carrying to the formerly remote communities of the foothills of the Himalaya a series of economical, political and social transformations unthinkable only few decades before.

The Naxi, living in territories easily accessible, were in the forefront of all these changes. Their culture was shattered once and again along the political reforms carried on during the 20th century. Many of the beliefs and traditions that the Naxi preserved until some decades ago, are disappearing quickly; others are suffering deep changes, and it is impossible to venture if they will have in the future the same importance to Naxi lives and values, as the economic development and the outside influences are eroding the same roots of their culture and religion.

Changes in the way of life lead the people to lose the references to which most of their old culture is related. The introduction of modern medicine changed forever the traditional concept of sickness, as well as the pivotal role of the Dongba in Naxi communities; the generalization of curriculum education make them forget ancient uses and folkways; the commoditization of the most outstanding characteristics of their culture carries the danger to make them forget the original meaning of their most sacred concepts in the past. The disappearance of the old wooden cabins take with it all the symbolism related to them; the heaven prop, the sacred hearth, the Sv basket; all are elements more and more difficult to find in the Naxi area. With the loss of these important symbols, it is possible that the beliefs regarding their connections with heaven, with the lands they inhabit, with their ancestral culture and the Sv life god, always present in their traditional life, could be lost in one generation of two.

What remains of the Naxi culture in the first years of the 21st century?

Amid the turbulent waters of political change and global modernization, during all these years the Naxi have cherished a sentiment that related their lives to one land and a common heritage. While in the more isolated villages many of the traditional elements of their culture can still be found, and are even carefully transmitted and preserved, in the most cosmopolitan centers, where outside influences are present on a daily basis, there is a secular respect for nature and its soul, a continuous worship of the spirit of the ancestors, a growing pride to belong to the only culture that has a pictographic scrip in use, a passion for arts, whatever being its expression, with music, dance and painting being an integral part of the life of every Naxi, and a conscience of the need to preserve an heritage that they know is unique in our world: Naxi traditional culture.

Bibliography

Allanic, Bernard. *La Voie Blanche: entre Chine et Tibet*. La Digitale. 1994.

Bacot, J. *Les Mo-so – Ethnographie des Mo-so, leurs religions, leur langue et leur ecriture*. Brill. Leiden. 1913.

Bai Gengsheng. *What is symbolized by the "Battle between Black and White?* In Guo Dalie and Yang Shiguang. Research on Naxi Dongba Culture (Dongba wenhua lun). Yunnan Peoples Press. Kunming. 1991.

Bai Gengsheng. Naxi zu fengshu zhi (*The folklore of the Naxi Nationality*). Central University of Nationalities Publishing House. Beijing. 2001.

Ceinos Arcones, Pedro. *El Matriarcado en China: Madres, Reinas, Diosas y Chamanes*. Miraguano. 2011.

Chao, Emily. *Layered Alterities: Discourses of the Other in Lijiang, China*. Concentric: Literary and Cultural Studies 34.2. September 2008: 101-120.

Chavannes, Edouard. *Documents historiques et geographiques relatives a Li-Kiang*. T'oung pao.

Chen Lie. Dongba Ji tian wenhua (*The culture of Worship Heaven among the Dongba*). Yunnan Peoples Press. 2000.

Chen Lie. *Foreword*. In Ge Agan. Ji tian gu ge (Old songs to worship heaven). China Popular Arts Press. 1988.

Debon, Juliette. *Dongba Pictographs and Dongba Modern Painting*. In Abstracts of theses. Academic conference of the

1999 Lijiang International Dongba Culture and Arts Festival. 1999.

Dennys, N.B. *Folklore of China and Its Affinities with That of the Aryan and Semitic Races.* 1870

Duncan. *Worship of the family God – the wedding ritual of "Suzhu".* 2011. In www.sinoglot.com/naxi/scrip-ture/worship-of-the-family-god-the-wedding-ritual-of-suzhu/

Duncan. *Dongba Dance.* 2010a. www.sinoglot.com/na-xi/dance/dongba-dance/

Duncan. *Dongba time divination.* 2010b. Www.sinoglot.com/naxi/scripture/dongba-time-divination-part-1-method/

Durremberger. Paul E. *Lisu Religion.* Northern Illinois University. 1989

EROC (*Encyclopedia of the Original Religions of China*). Zhonguo Yuanshi zongjiao baike quanshu. Chengdu. 2003.

Fang Guoli and He Zhiwu. Naxi xiangxing wenzi pu (*Manual of the Naxi pictographic script*). Yunnan Peoples Press. Kunming. 2005.

Feuchtwang, Stephan. *Popular Religion in China. The Imperial Metaphor.* Curzon. 2001

Gao Lishi. Dai zu "longlin" chongbai dui shengdai gongxian huanbao (*Contribution of the sacred forests of the Dai to the protection of nature*). In "Dai zu wenhua lun" (Discussions about Dai culture) Yunnan Nationalities Press. Kunming. 2000.

Ge Agan. Dongba shenxi yu Dongba wupu (*The system of gods of the Dongba and the genealogy of their dance*). Kunming. 1992.

Goodman, Jim. *Children of the Jade Dragon: The Naxi of Lijiang and Their Mountain Neighbours the Yi*. Asia Film House. 1997.

Guo Dalie. Naxi zu fengqing lu (*Naxi Nationality Folklore*). Sichuan Nationalities Press. 1998.

Guo Dalie. *The Constitution of Dongba culture*. In Guo Dalie y Yang Shiguang. Research in Naxi Dongba Culture. 1991.

Guo Dalie and Bai Gengshen. *Abstracts of Theses The 1999 International Academic Conference of Lijiang Dongba Culture and Arts Festival*. Lijiang. 1999.

Guo Dalie and He Zhiwu. Naxi zu shi (*History of the Naxi Nationality*). Sichuan nationalities Press. 1994.

Guo Dalie and Yang Shiguang. *Research on Naxi Dongba Culture* (Dongba wenhua lun). Yunnan Peoples Press. Kunming. 1991.

Guo Dalie and Yang Shiguang. *Research on Naxi Dongba Culture* (Dongba wenhua lunji). Yunnan Peoples Press. Kunming, 1985.

Guo Dalie and Zheng Weidong. *Proverbs of the Naxi Nationality*. Yunnan Nationality Press. 1998.

He Baolin. Yuangu liulai de shenquan – Dongba wenhua yu naxi zu. (*Coming from an old sacred fountain – Dongba culture and Naxi nationality*). Yunnan Nationalities Press. 2000.

He Baolin. Naxi xiangxing wenzi shiyong zhujie (*Notes for the use of the Naxi pictographic writing*). Yunnan Peoples Press. Kunming. 2007.

He Jiren and Jiang Zhuyi. Naxi yu jian zhi (*Brief introduction to Naxi language*). Nationalities Press. Beijing. 1985.

He Jiren and He Zhiwu. *Research on the dialects and social history of the Naxi nationality*. In Researches on the social history of the Naxi nationality volume 3. Yunnan Nationalities Press. 1988.

He Limin. Dongba wen yuan yu jinsha jiang yanhui (*The origin of Dongba script and the rock paintings of the Jinsha River*). In Zhao Shihong. Dongba wenhua yanjiu suo lunwen xuanji (Selected papers from the office of research on the Dongba culture). Yunnan Nationalities Press. 2003.

He Limin. Cong "Chuangshiji" kan gudai Naxi zu shehui (*Viewing the old culture of the Naxi in the Creation of the World*). In Guo Dalie and Yang Shiguang. Research on Naxi Dongba Culture (Dongba wenhua lunji). Yunnan Peoples Press. Kunming. 1985.

He Limin and He Shicheng. *The Dto-mba ceremony to Propitiate the Demons of Suicide*. In Oppitz and Hsu. Naxi and Moso Ethnography. Kin, Rites, Pictographs. Zurich. 1998.

He Pinzheng. *Naxi Dongba Pictographic Dictionary*. Yunnan Fine Arts Publishing House. Kunming. 2004.

He Pingzheng. Lijiang gu naxi ren de minsu jieqing yu yuanshi zongjiao de guanxi (*Popular festivals of the Naxi of Lijiang and its relation with their original religion*). In Zhao Shihong. Dongba wenhua yanjiu suo lunwen xuanji (Selected papers of the Office of Research on the Dongba Culture). Yunnan Nationalities Press. 2003. Pp 305-315.

He Pingzheng y He Zhongze. *Naxi Nationality and Dongba Culture*. China Nationalities Photographic Art Press. 1999.

He Shangli. *Sacred Place of Baishui Mesa*. Peoples Fine Arts Publishing. 2000.

He Shaoying. Naxi zu wenhua shi (*A cultural history of the Naxi nationality*). Yunnan Nationalities Press. Kunming. 2001.

He Yunfeng. Naxi zu yinyue shi (*History of the music of the Naxi nationality*). Central Academy of Music Press. Beijing. 2004.

He Zhaowu and Peng Gang. *A Critical History of Classical Chinese Philosophy*. New World Press. 2009.

He Zhiwu. Jinqu xiangshang de Naxi zu. (*Enterprising and progressive Naxi nationality*). Yunnan Youth Publishing House. 1987.

He Zhiwu. Naxi Dongba wenhua (*Naxi Dongba culture*). Jilin Education Publishing House. 1989

He Zhiwu. Ji feng yishi ji mupai huapu (*Painted woods in the ceremony to worship the wind*). Yunnan Peoples Press. 1992.

He Zhiwu and Yang Fuquan. Zhongguo yuanshi zongjiao ziliao congbian – Naxi zu juan. (*Source books on the primitive religions of China – Naxi volume*). Shanghai Peoples Press. 1993.

He Zhonghua and He Shangli. Naxi Dongba shendi minjian wenxue xuan (*Selected popular literature of the sacred place of the Naxi Dongba*). Yunnan Nationalities Press. 1991.

Hsu, Elizabeth. *Introduction*. In Oppitz and Hsu. Naxi and Moso Ethnography. Kin, Rites, Pictographs. Zurich. 1998.

Jackson, Anthony. *Nakhi Religion: An Analytical Appraisal of the Na-khi Ritual Texts*. Mouton, The Hague. 1976.

Jackson, Anthony. *Tibetan Bon Rites in China*: A Case of Cultural Diffusion. In James F. Fisher. Himalayan Anthropology. Mouton, 1978.

Jackson, Anthony and Pan Anshi. *Authors of Naxi ritual books, Index books and books of Divination*. In Oppitz and Hsu. Naxi and Moso Ethnography. Kin, Rites, Pictographs. Zurich. 1998.

Kuiper, Kathleen. *The Culture of China*. Britannica Educational Publishing. 2011.

Kurosawa, Naomichi. *Fundamental Research on the text of Naxi Dongba script – Extraction of a framework based on frequency and appearance of pictographs*. 2009. Abstract in www.xiulong.it

Lee, Bruce. *Naxi Paper*. Yunnan Fine Arts Publishing. 2003.

Lewis, Paul, and Bai Bibo. *Hani Cultural Themes*. White Lotus. 2002.

Li Guowen. Renshen zhimou - Dongba jishi mianmian guan (*Mediators between men and gods – A view of every aspect of the Dongba priests*). Yunnan Peoples Press. 1993.

Li Guowen. *Dongba culture dictionary*. Yunnan Education Publishing House. 1997.

Li Jinchun. *Etnia Naxi de la región de Lijiang*. En Yan Ruxian. Matrimonio y familia de las etnias minoritarias de China. Beijing. 1991.

Li Jingshen. *"Ssugv" ritual and its social function*. In Guo Dalie and Yang Shiguang. Research on Naxi Dongba culture. Kunming. 1991.

Li Jingshen. Naxi dongba wen de chuangzhi ji qita (*About the creation of Naxi Dongba characters and other matters*). In Zhao Shihong. Dongba wenhua yanjiu suo lunwen xuanji (Selectes papers from the office of research on the Dongba culture). Yunnan Nationalities Press. 2003.

Li Pingping. *Typological Transformation of Courtyard House in Lijiang Area: Women and Nuclear Space of Naxi Dwelling*. Unpublished PhD Thesis of the University of Hong Kong. 2005.

Li Xi. *A road close to the gods- Dongba painting, "The road to heaven" of the Naxi people*. Peoples Fine Arts Publishing. 2001.

Li Xi. *The Baisha Frescoes in Lijiang County.* Sichuan Peoples Press. Chengdu. 1999.

Li Xi and A Yuan. *The Dongba Culture of the Naxi.* Linnan Fine Arts Press. 1998.

Liu Xiangxiao. *Is Dongba Religion a Branch of Bon?* In Guo Dalie and Yang Shiguang. Research on Naxi Dongba Culture. Kunming. 1991.

Ma Yin (ed.). *China's National Minorities.* Foreign Languages Press. Beijing. 1989.

Maspero, Henri. *La société et la religion des Chinois anciens et celles des Tai moderns.* Gallimard. 1929.

Mathieu, Christine. *A history and Anthropological study of the ancient kingdoms of the Sino-Tibetan borderland- Naxi and Moso.* Mellen Press. 2003.

Mathieu, Christine and Ho, Cindy. *Quentin Roosevelt's China Ancestral Realms of the Naxi.* Rubin Museum of Art/ Arnoldsche Art Publishers. 2011.

McKhann, Charles. *Naxi, Rerkua, Moso, Meng: Kinship, Politics and Ritual on the Yunnan Sichuan Frontier.* In Oppitz and Hsu. Naxi and Moso Ethnography. Kin, Rites, Pictographs. Zurich, 1998.

McKhann, Charles. *The Naxi and the Nationalities Question.* In Stevan Harrell (ed.), Cultural Encounters on China's Ethnic Frontiers. University of Washington Press. Seattle. 1995.

McKhann, Charles. *Fleshing out the Bones: The Cosmic and Social Dimensions of Space in Naxi Architecture.* In Chien Chiao and Nicholas Tapp (eds.). Ethnicity and Ethnic Groups in China, New Asia Academic Bulletin, v.8, The Chinese University, Hong Kong. 1989.

Michaud, Alexis. *Pictographs and the language of Naxi rituals*. In Mathieu and Ho. Quentin Roosevelt's China. Ancestral Realms of the Naxi. 2011.

Mikio Miyamoto. *Guiding the Soul to the Land of the Dead*. http://nierika.web.infoseek.co.jp/so-konroe.htm. Accessed 6 Nov 2011.

Mu Lichun. *A Brief Account of the Social Status of Dongba*. In Guo Dalie and Yang Shiguang. Research on Naxi Dongba Culture. Yunnan Peoples Press. Kunming. 1991.

Mu Lichun. Dongba wenhua jiemi (*The Dongba culture unveiled*). Yunnan Peoples Press. Kunming. 2005.

Office of Publication and organization of old documents of the minorities of Yunnan. *Translation of the main old documents of the Dongba Naxi*. Kunming. 1989.

Oppitz, Michael. *The Propitiation of Heaven*. In Oppitz, Michael and Hsu, Elisabeth. Naxi and Moso Ethnography: Kin, Rites, Pictographs. Volkerdemuseum. Zurich. 1998.

Oppitz, Michael and Hsu, Elisabeth. *Naxi and Moso Ethnography: Kin, Rites, Pictographs*. Volkerdemuseum. Zurich. 1998.

Outlook of the Naxi culture (Naxi zu wenhua daguan). Yunnan Nationalities Press. Kunming. 1999.

Pan Anshi. *The translation of Naxi religious texts*. In Oppitz, Michael and Hsu, Elisabeth. Naxi and Moso Ethnography: Kin, Rites, Pictographs. Volkerdemuseum. Zurich. 1998.

People's Government of Lijiang Naxi Autonomous County. *China's Lijiang Naxi ancient music*. Lijiang. (No date).

Pinson, Jacqueline. *What you can't see is Medicine - Naxi culture through American eyes*. Yunnan Nationalities Press. 2006.

254

Rees, Helen. *Echoes of history: Naxi music in modern China.* Oxford University Press. 2000.

Rock, Joseph F. *Banishing the Devil of Disease among the Nashi: Weird Ceremonies Performed by an Aboriginal Tribe in the Heart of Yunnan Province, China.* 1924.

Rock, Joseph F. *The Na-khi Naga cults and related ceremonies.* In. M. E. O. Rome. 1952.

Rock, Joseph F. *The Muan Bpo ceremony or the Sacrifice to heaven as practiced by the Na-khi.* Monumenta Serica, vol, XIII, 1- 1948.

Rock. Joseph F. *Studies on Nakhi Literature.* Bulletin de l'Ecole francaise d'Extreme-Orient. 1937.

Rock. Joseph. F. *Romance of K'a-ma-gyu-mi-gkyi.* Bulletin de l'Ecole francaise d'Extreme-Orient. 1939.

Rock, Joseph. F. *The ancient Nakhi Kingdom of Southwest China.* Harvard University Press. 1947.

Rock, Joseph F. *A Na-khi – English Encyclopedic dictionary.* In. M. E. O. Vol I. Roma. 1963. Vol II. Roma. 1972.

Roosevelt. Quentin Roosevelt's China: Ancestral Realms of the Naxi May 13, 2011 – September 19, 2011 [4th floor] Wall Guide, Audio Tour, and Checklist Images

Sangde Nuowa (He Yunfeng). *Ritual Music Helalekou and Worere of Dongba: An Insider's Report.*

Stutley, Margaret. *Shamanism: An Introduction.* Rouledge. 2002

Sun Hongkai. *The Nationalities of the six valleys and their language branches.* In Minzu Xuebao, Kunming. 1983.

Sun Hongkai. *The Ersu Shaba pictographic writing.* Asian Highlands Perspectives. 1 (2009), 159-186.

Tacon et al.. *Naturalism, Nature and Questions of Style in Jinsha River Rock Art, Northwest Yunnan, China*. Cambridge Archeological Journal 20:1, 67-86. 2010

Vannicelli, Luigi. *La religion dei Lolo*. Milano. 1946.

Wang Zhushen. *The Jingpo: Kachin of the Yunnan Plateau*. F.K. Lehman. 1997

Wu Xueyuan. *A Brief Study of the Structure and Form of Dongba Chanting Music*. In Abstracts of theses. Academic conference of the 1999 Lijiang International Dongba Culture and Arts Festival. 1999.

Xi Yuhua. *Shu: Naxi Nature Goddess Archetype*. In Gender relations in forest societies in Asia: patriarchy at odds. By Govind Kelkar, Dev Nathan, Pierre Gilbert Walter. 2002

Xi Yuhua. *Naxi women and folk divination*. In Abstracts of theses. Academic conference of the 1999 Lijiang International Dongba Culture and Arts Festival. 1999.

Xiu Long. *Musiche e danze Naxi*. www.xiulong.it/pubbl/musicadanzeNaxi.pdf. Accessed 2011, Nov 5th.

Xu Ji. You Lijiang, xue Naxi yu (*Study Naxi language for traveling in Lijiang*). Yunnan Nationalities Press. Kunming. 2003.

Xuan Ke. *Music Comes from Horror*. In Abstracts of theses. Academic conference of the 1999 Lijiang International Dongba Culture and Arts Festival. 1999.

Yang Fuquan. *Ethnographic Papers of Yang Fuquan on the Naxi Ethnic Group*. China Books Publishers. 2008.

Yang Fuquan. *Mentorship of Indigenous Cultural Specialists. A case Studio of Training of Dongba, Naxi Priests*. In Xu Jianchu and Stephen Mikesell. Landscapes of Diversity: Indigenous Knowledge, Sustainable livelihoods and Resource Governance in Montane Mainland Southeast Asia. Kunming. Yunnan Science and Technology Press. 2003.

Yang, Fuquan. *The Epistemological Concept of Nature Conservation and Human Activities as seen from the Dongba Religion of Naxi People of Southwest China*. Paper for the Bridging Scales and Epistemologies Conference. Alexandria. Egypt. 2004.

Yang Fuquan. *Naxi Women and Natural Resources*. In Indigenous Asia: Knowledge, technology and gender relations. 1998.

Yang Fuquan. *Reflections on the relationship between Na Mu Ji and the Naq ethnic groups*. In He Ming and Li Zhinong. Review of Anthropology and Ethnology in Southwest China. Social Sciences Academic Press. Beijing. 2009.

Yang Fuquan. *The SSu life gods and their cults*. In Oppitz, Michael and Hsu, Elisabeth. Naxi and Moso Ethnography: Kin, Rites, Pictographs. Volkerdemuseum. Zurich. 1998.

Yang Fuquan. Hun lu (*The souls way*). Haitian publishers. Shenzhen. 2000.

Yang Fuquan. Shenshan xia guguo- zuojin naxi ren de xinling he jiayuan (*An old kingdom under the sacred mountain- entering the soul and the garden of the Naxi people*). Yunnan Nationalities Press. 1999.

Zamblera, Stefano. *Les signes d'animaux et de creatures mythiques en Orient et en Occident – Creatures mythiques anima-les dans les manuscrits naxis*. www.xiulong.it/Dongba-/conferences/les-signes-danimaux-et-de-creatures-mythiques-en-orient-et-en-occident/ Accessed 21 Dec 2011.

Zamblera, Stefano. Appunti di studio sulla storia dell\'etnia Naxi e della frequentazione umana nella regione di Lijiang. xiulong.it/Dongba/storia/storianaxi.xml. Accessed 21 dec 2011.

Zhang Chunyan and He Yong. *The wondrous Lijiang*. Yunnan Technological Press. Kunming. 2005.

Zhang Songquan. *Lijiang and the Naxi People*. In "The Yunnan ethnic groups and their cultures". Yunnan Peoples Press. Kunming. 2000.

Zhang Weiwen and Zeng Qingnan. *In search of China's minorities*. New World Press. Beijing, 1993.

Zhang Xu. *A Naxi Cremation Ceremony*. In Oppitz, Michael and Hsu, Elisabeth. Naxi and Moso Ethnography: Kin, Rites, Pictographs. Volkerdemuseum. Zurich. 1998.

Zhao Xingwen. *Naxi Dances*. In Chen Weiye, Ji Lanwei and Ma Wei. Flying Dragon and Dancing Phoenix – An introduction to selected Chinese Minority Folk Dances. New World Press. Beijing. 1987.

Zhao Zhenxiu. Dongba xiangxing wen changyong zici yizhu (*Translation of the most common Dongba pictographs*). Yunnan Peoples Press. Kunming. 1998.

Zheng Tongsheng. *The old town of Lijiang*. 2001.

Zhu Liangwen, Shi Kehui and Sun Ruyan. *Folk Residences in Lijiang, Yunnan*. In Wang Zhili. Chinese Traditional Residential Architecture. Shandong Science and Technology Press. Jinan, 1998.

Glossary

Arranged mainly according to their pinyin transliterations, with other variants included.

Alili: One of the most famous and popular dances of the Naxi, daily performed in Lijiang and other places.

Baba: A kind of flat bread usually made of wheat with a salty or sweet filling.

Baxhishile: Music of Baisha, a long pacifist elegy.

Bimo: Traditional priest of the Yi that live east of the Naxi. They use books written in a syllabic language. Older denomination of the Naxi ritual specialists, also called biuq.

Chamu: Old dance notations of the Naxi.

Ch'er: A kind of local bacon.

Congrenlien: Charelien. The first post-flood ancestor of the Naxi; he is continuously referred to in their myths and rituals. His name is transcribed as Ts'o-za-llu-ghugh in Rock's texts and scholars that base their works in Rock's researches.

Cunhongbaobai. Also Cunhongbaobaiming. The celestial female ancestor of the Mu kings and human beings, she is the daughter of the heavenly god Zhilao Apu.

Dongba: Dto-mba, dtomba. Originally referred to the priests that chant their scriptures. Later it was used to designate also the scriptures (Dongba Classics), the script in which the scriptures are written (Dongba script), the individual pictographs (Dongba pictographs), the system of beliefs preserved in these scriptures (Dongba religion), and being the most outstanding part of the Naxi culture, it is used also as a synonym of it, and we heard about Dongba culture, Dongba traditions, etc., when people refers in fact to Naxi culture or Naxi traditions.

Dongba Shiluo: The patriarch of Dongba Tradition, the first mediator between human beings and the gods. He is a local transformation of the Bon ancestor with whom shares many of his characteristics.

Dongjing: Religious music of Chinese origin adopted b the elites of some districts of Yunnan, especially famous among the Naxi due to perfection that reached among them before 1949, and the resurgence in the present times. It has become an ethnic marker of the Naxi.

Ds-ler: Flat metal bell with a beetle, used by the Dongba at ceremonies. To it are tied a white or blue colored piece of silk and the claw of an eagle or blood pheasant.

Dsola: Divination books of the Naxi.

Duoge: Celestial warriors.

Duoma: Figurines of gods or demons made of dough or clay used in the Donba ceremonies.

Geba: The syllabic script of the Naxi.

Hami: Goddess.

Harlalluku: Ceremony to propitiate the wind demons especially performed after the suicide of a family member.

Hazhiphi: Road to heaven scroll. A scroll used in funerary ceremonies to guide the souls of the deceased through the punishments for the sins committed during their lives, to the paradise.

Ko: Five lobed crown the Dongba wear when performing their ceremonies, related to their supposed domain over the five directions.

K'o-byo: Wooden slats used at Dongba ceremonies, to represent gods or demons. These latter are truncated, the others wedge-shaped.

Lijiang: Likiang, Lichiang. The main city of the Naxi; seat of the Mu kings and Chinese administrations, it is their economic, political and cultural center. Called Dayan by the Naxi. Sadham by the Tibetans.

Llubhu: Leebus. Naxi shamans, originally only women can be llubhu, later most of them were men.

Lulu: Name given to some populations in Tacheng. Officially considered Naxi they show some differences in language, marriage and funerary rituals. Some writers consider that they are the product of the blending of Lisu and Naxi populations.

Moso: Moso, or Mo-so, was the traditional denomination of the Naxi. In the last years is used to name the Na or eastern Naxi, who insist in consider themselves a different ethnic entity than the "proper" Naxi.

Naheng: Naxi people living in Baishuitai, usually considered the purest of their race

Naxi: Term adopted in 1954 to designate the ethnic group previously known as Nakhi, Na-khi, or Mo-so in the western ethnography and with names related to Moso, Moxie, among the Chinese history documents. The nowadays Moso or Mosuo people, called Na in their own language, retained the traditional Chinese appellation to mark the difference with the Naxi, to whom they do not consider to be related.

Nv: The body of the deceased is represented as a pine branch into which eyes, mouth, etc., have been carved, called Nv, later preserved in a cave near the village.

Paq: Ancient woman diviners.

Pumi: One of the officially recognized national minorities, it is though that they are the descendants of the P'u or Pu peoples that inhabited Lijiang area before the arrival of the forefathers of the Naxi, and that, defeated, slowly retired to mountainous areas. Also known as Boa, Xifang, Primi.

Remeicuo: Primitive funeral song and dance of the Naxi.

Rerke: Yuanke or Ruarke, One of the branches of the Naxi inhabiting the area around Baidi.

Sashakou: The name of the procedure to send the dead to heaven, it involves inserting a red pack, made of silk or paper with certain grains of rice, some tea leaves, and few small pieces of gold and silver into the dying person's mouth before his or her last breath

Sanduo: Ssa-do, Sa-ddo. Protector deity of the Naxi, the spirit of the Yulong Mountain, he is worshipped on Feb 8th.

Shu: Nature god. There are many Shu nature gods. A concept related to the Tibetan Klu, the Hindu naga and the Chinese Dragon.

Sv: Also Ssu. The Sv life god of a family resides in the Sv basket. The individual Sv life gods can separate from this common spirit at the wedding of the daughters and at death.

Tusi: Local indigenous rulers that governed the minority and frontier peoples during the dynastic era. They enjoyed great autonomy, were backed by imperial power, and had the duty of sending the timely tributes, assisting the imperial administration and recognizing the imperial sovereignty over their territories.

Yuma: Celestial guardians whose images are usually hung in houses and ritual places.

Zhao: Kingdoms, statelets of northwest Yunnan.

Zherkhin: One of the branches of the Naxi inhabiting the low lands of the Yangtze loop. This name means "inhabitants of the hot lands.